CROSSOVER CHILDREN

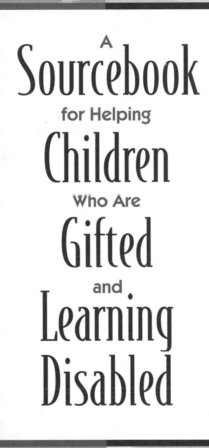

A
Sourcebook
for Helping
Children
Who Are
Gifted
and
Learning
Disabled

Second Edition · **Marlene Bireley**

Published by The Council for Exceptional Children

Library of Congress Cataloging-in-Publication Data

Bireley, Marlene.
   Crossover children : a sourcebook for helping children who are
gifted and learning disabled / Marlene Bireley. — 2nd ed.
    p.   cm.
  Includes bibliographical references (p. 1).
  ISBN 0-86586-264-8 (pbk.)
  1. Learning disabled children—Education. 2. Gifted children-
-Education. I. Title.
LC4704.5.B57   1995
371.9—dc20   95-23133
                                           CIP

ISBN 0-86586-264-8

Copyright 1995 by The Council for Exceptional Children, 1920 Association
Drive, Reston, Virginia 22091-1589

Stock No. P5121

Printed in the United States of America

10 9 8 7 6 5 4 3 2

To the crossover children and their families
whose courage and need demanded that this book be written.

Acknowledgments

No book is written by one person. I may have put the words on the paper, but the genesis of those words came from many sources. I would particularly like to thank my friends and colleagues Marlin Languis, Ted Williamson, and Lilburn Hoehn, who collaborated on various studies that greatly enhanced my understanding of the crossover condition. Grateful thanks as well to my friends Marsha Schubert, Denise Boldman, Sue Amidon, Eileen Reser, and Fran Landers, who read parts of the manuscript and offered excellent advice on changes that needed to be made. Thanks also to Bonnie Mathies, who provided information about appropriate computer programs.

I am enormously indebted to my professional colleagues throughout the state of Ohio who found crossover children and sent them or information about them to me. Finally, thanks to the children and their families who shared their stories and their time knowing that the outcome would likely benefit others more than themselves. We all admire your dedication and your courage and hope that your most cherished dreams will be fulfilled.

About the Author

Marlene Bireley has spent over 35 years in education as an elementary school teacher, special education teacher, school psychologist, and university professor. In 1969, she joined the faculty of Wright State University as Coordinator of Special Education. In that capacity, she developed programs in special education, gifted education, and school psychology. Since her early retirement in 1988, she has continued to teach, write, and consult in these three areas. In addition, she has maintained a private practice in psychology specializing in exceptional children. She co-edited *Understanding the Gifted Adolescent: Educational, Developmental, and Multicultural Issues* with Judy Genshaft and *Serving Gifted and Talented Students: A Resource for School Personnel* with Dr. Genshaft and Constance Hollinger.

Preface

PURPOSES AND PATTERNS: THE WHY AND HOW OF THIS BOOK

This is a book about a group of children whose existence is unrecognized by some and denied by others. But they are real and they are in need of our help. Most of the literature available refers to them as learning disabled/gifted or gifted/learning disabled children. I have chosen to use the term *crossover children* because their characteristics and their needs truly cross over between the categories known as gifted and learning disabled. If we try to fit them into either mold, to some extent we will fail.

My own interest in children with learning disabilities goes back to my graduate education, when we were just beginning to recognize and serve students who were then labeled "neurologically handicapped," now "learning disabled." I brought to that same graduate education a lifelong interest in gifted students stemming from my own childhood experiences as a "grade skipper" and academically able student. Those two interests, combined with more than 35 years of experience as a teacher, psychologist, and university professor, have culminated in the study of crossover children described in this book.

Crossover Children is written for many people. I hope that the readers are regular class teachers, teachers of learning disabled and gifted students, school psychologists, counselors, administrators, and parents. I have balanced readability with inclusion of some of the research and knowledge base from which my conclusions have sprung. The bibliography in Appendix D contains the body of knowledge I have used to supplement my own clinical work. In my experience with special education, gifted education, and school psychology I have found that questions raised by one of these groups have often been answered in the literature of the other. I have synthesized information from these groups that is pertinent to crossover children for the purpose of providing guidelines for a better education and therefore better opportunities for this group.

The unique problems of the child who is both gifted and has learning disabilities stem from the unlikely juxtaposition of the two conditions. The parents of a child who has obviously good intelligence are devastated when that child fails to make normal academic gains or is labeled a behavior problem as soon as "student" conduct is expected. The greatest danger lies in overlooking the gifts in the rush to overcome the disability. We have a tendency to become that which we are labeled, the so-called "self-fulfilling prophecy." If a child is perceived and perceives himself or herself as disabled *that* is what he or she will become. If the child's self-concept is that of a person with both ability *and* disability, that very belief will strengthen and assist him or her in overcoming whatever problems exist. If this book has an overriding theme, that is it.

CONTENT OF THE BOOK

For the most part, this is a "how to do it" book. It is concerned with instructional content and practice. Consistent with CEC's common core of knowledge and skills, the book looks at different learning styles and provides suggestions on how to adapt teaching to these styles. Included are suggestions on how to select, adapt, and use instructional strategies and materials according to characteristics of the crossover learner. It shows how to teach students to use problem solving, and other cognitive strategies to meet their individual needs. It also helps the reader better understand the characteristics of these special learners and the effects their exceptional condition may have on their lives. I have provided a planning guide for educational programming for these children. I have summarized the best ideas I could find on dealing with the immediate social/behavioral, enrichment, and intervention needs of the crossover child, as well as the need to plan for life after high school. I have added several Appendixes that list resources from which more assistance or more detailed information can be obtained. As the subtitle of the book indicates, this is a sourcebook. The serious reader will need to look elsewhere for additional ideas once the most pressing problems of an individual child have been determined.

A final word on style. I have chosen, when it seems absolutely necessary, to use the pronoun "he" to refer to the crossover child and "she" to refer to the classroom teacher. I, as you, am uncomfortable with these stereotypes. However, it is true that the majority of crossover children are boys and most of their elementary teachers are female. When appropriate, I have deviated from this form by switching pronouns or by using the cumbersome he/she. It is my hope that, whatever the style, the ideas contained on the following pages will assist you in providing a more fulfilling educational and life experience for the crossover children in your professional or personal care.

Marlene Bireley

Table of Contents

Acknowledgments iv

About the Author v

Preface vii

1. **Introducing the Crossover Concept 1**
   Other Real People 3
   The Crossover Profile 5
   Summary 6

2. **Educational Planning and Programming 9**
   Tips for Parents 9
   Tips for Educators 12
   Programming for the Crossover Child 13
   Summary 15

3. **Behavioral and Social Interventions 17**
   Controlling Impulsivity 18
     Meichenbaum's Cognitive-Behavioral Modification
       and *Think Aloud* 18
     Kendall's *Stop and Think* 19
     Behavioral strategies 19
     Personalizing behavior management   19
   Controlling Disorganization 20
   Increasing Attention 21
     Classroom interventions 23
   Enhancing Memory 24
     Specific memory aids 25
   Increasing Social Skills 26
     Social skills training 27
   Developing a Positive Self-Concept 27
   Controlling Socially Inappropriate Behaviors 29
     Verbal bullying 29
     Perfectionism 29
     "I want to be like everyone else" 30
   Summary 31

4. Academic Intervention 33
The Relationship of Clinical Teaching and Cognitive
    Strategies Teaching 34
Selecting Specific Strategies 35
  Cognitive strategy sequences 35
Teaching Basic Skills 35
  Language arts 35
  Handwriting and spelling 41
  Mathematics 44
  Content Subjects 45
Summary 47

5. Academic Enrichment 51
Curriculum for the Gifted 51
Major Cognitive Operations 52
  Creative thinking 52
  Creative problem solving 53
  Decision-making skills 55
  Critical thinking 56
  Other thinking skills 58
  Inductive, deductive, and analogic reasoning 60
Published Programs for Teaching Thinking 60
Technology and Thinking 62
The Integrative Education Model 62
Summary 64

6. Crossover Children Grow Up 67
Vulnerabilities of the Crossover Adolescent 68
  Needs related to learning disability 68
  Needs related to giftedness 69
Career Choice and Postsecondary Education 70
  Learning style and career choice 70
Postsecondary Choices 71
  Four-year colleges and universities 72
  Alternatives to 4-year colleges 76
The Crossover Adult 77
Summary 77

Appendixes

**A Journals and Publishing Companies with Resources
for Students Who Are Gifted and Learning Disabled 81**

**B Organizations that Serve Students Who Are Gifted
or Learning Disabled 85**

C Elementary and Secondary Computer Programs 87

**D A Bibliography on the Crossover Condition and
Related Issues 91**

1

Introducing the Crossover Concept

It is fitting to begin this book with a reflection from a real crossover individual. His story dramatically illustrates the importance of determining early that a child is a crossover and meeting his or her needs appropriately. The young man wrote the following as his college admissions essay. He is now attending a prestigious university where he is pursuing his dream of becoming a professional musician. He has given permission to print this with the hope that others may receive what he was denied for such a long time.

I took on a greater responsibility than that of any other student in twelve years of school. I took on a greater role that needed a perfect performance everyday. I was a natural. My role was not easy to live up to on a daily basis, but I always tried my best. It all started in second grade. I set a new record for most minutes spent in the corner with my nose against the wall. In the second grade the corner had become almost like a second home for me. Yes, I was the class clown. I always entertained my fellow classmates. They all loved me for it. I was a hit. All through elementary school and into junior high school, I was always reminded of how easily I was distracted, of how often I distracted others. Every year I had a teacher who, as it seemed, read from a script that was passed down to one another that outlined my "behavior problem." It was like a broken record, "Why do you waste all your talent and time on trying so hard to be a clown? You have so much potential (I hated that word) and no self-discipline to actually do anything about it. What is wrong with you?"

What was wrong with me? It still makes me wonder why the professionals who were supposed to know the answers to questions like these asked *me,* a ten year old, for the answer. Time and time again I was sent to the principal or to the guidance counselor so we could together figure out what my problem was with school. I went through years of teachers trying to help and giving up on me before I finally had my question answered. I was always looked at as a talented, intelligent kid who had little self-respect except for my music talent and no desire to accomplish anything in school. So, as the theory went, "If he does not care about his own life, why should we?"

The drama continued into high school. My first two years of high school were filled with the same sort of pep talks, lectures, and condescending statements, obviously aimed either to hurt my feelings or to give me a nasty guilt trip. I will never forget my tenth grade math teacher. I had just completed a test in his class. I handed the test in before anyone else. He said to me, "It figures you would be the first to hand your test in. After all, you don't do your homework, you don't stop talking, you are easily distracted. You probably failed this test miserably." Well, I ended up staying after school so he could quickly mark my exam and rub the results in. I ended up getting a high B on the exam. He responded to the good result by getting very frustrated and angry. (I observed that all through school teachers hated kids that never did homework, had bad behavior, and never cracked a book, but still aced their tests.) He responded by telling me that I would amount to nothing in life, that he had checked up on me and found that I had a long history of this kind of behavior that would keep me from doing anything. Although this teacher seemed to dislike me, my guidance counselor, and other teachers put me in honor classes that were supposed to keep me challenged and "on the ball." While I did try to work hard, my disorganization and lack of concentration always got in the way. I was labeled the guidance department's "underachiever of the year." It made me proud. Pretty good for the reigning class clown who entertained his way to the sophomore class presidency.

As I look back on my first two years of high school, I find that getting straight Bs my freshman year and Cs my sophomore year was not too shabby, considering everything else that was going on—or not going on. I wonder what kind of grades I could have gotten if my academic problems had been addressed early on instead of accusing me of being "care-free."

Act IV, *The Big Move.* I will never forget the day my father told me that the company was being sold and we were moving to Ohio. I responded, "What, Idaho?" "No, no, Ohio," he said. Now when you grow up ten minutes out of New York City and you hear news like this, it is a catastrophe. Visions of farms, cows, and driving twenty miles to school every day popped into my head. Then visions of starting out at a new school my junior year were taking over. Will I make friends? Will my new school be small or large? So many questions. No choice in the matter at all. So, we were off. I got over my initial fear of Ohio when I saw some skyscrapers. Well, they did not quite touch the sky like the Empire State Building, but they were good enough. School started, and my other fears were settled as well. It took some time, but I made my friends. I got involved with the school. Certainly my music ability helped. It really was not all that bad.

Oh, but wait. Some other problems still existed, but they were much worse. Now, instead of *having* a reputation for my lack of study skills, I was *making* one. At my new school more students did better and were more serious about success so a person such as myself was not glorified. The competition at the high school was intense. All my friends got report cards that ranged from 3.5 to 4.2. I still had the same bad study habits, and teachers were always on my back just like before, but this time I was alone in many ways. My grades got worse my senior year, and by the time I finally got adjusted, serious health problems in my family had replaced concerns related to the move.

At this point I knew that all through school I had never lived up to the potential I had. I was upset about it, but nothing could be done. I finally graduated high school and went off to a college that I very soon discovered was not right for me. I went to college knowing that the problems I had had not been addressed. I knew I would probably have the same problems I had had during my first twelve years of school, but in a college setting. I decided I did not want that. After a week I came home from college in an effort to get help in the areas where I needed it. I entered and attended college near home while seeing an educational specialist who was trying to help me with my study skills.

Finale, *The Big Discovery*. It was amazing. The three people who were trying to help me with academic problems, personal problems and college concerns all said the same thing to me. "Have you ever been tested for Attention Deficit Disorder or any learning disabilities?" I would answer, "What? I did not hear you." They would respond, "Exactly." I told them it was highly doubtful, because I thought if that were the problem, it would have been discovered years ago by my previous teachers. I still decided, however, to go ahead and find out if that could possibly be true. I was diagnosed by a physician as having ADHD and was put on a mild dose of Ritalin. Immediately, the results were amazing. I was able to sit and work hard for hours at a time and not get tired or unfocused. This seemed like the answer. The only thing left to do was to take official tests for ADD and LD. I was tested by a highly recognized Ohio psychologist who discovered and observed that I was clearly an ADD student, and that, in addition, I had a mild learning disability in math. She said, "In the twelve years of school, somehow you were missed." I cannot describe how I felt when she told me that somehow I was *"missed."* I had mixed feelings. In one sense I kind of felt betrayed by every teacher, guidance counselor, and principal who for years had sat me down and yelled and lectured me in an effort to get through to me. Not once did they ever think about hyperactivity or LD. Was I supposed to ask to be tested for these things? I will never know why I was never considered for these problems. Was it my behavior problem that made teachers just give up on me? On a more happy note, I felt relieved. All of the years of trying so hard to do things that seemed so impossible for me to do were not a result of my laziness, lack of effort, or lack of concern for my future. There was a reason for my hyperactive behavior problem and my difficulties with math. I was not "just a bad kid" after all.

The more I think about it, the less I care about why I was a *"missed" child*. The important thing for me is to figure out where I go from here with this news. I now plan on finding the right college for me, getting a degree in music performance, and finally, in about five years, playing in a Broadway pit orchestra. I know that even though Ritalin will make a big difference for me, I will still have to work hard, perhaps harder than other students, to succeed in school. I know I will succeed. It was Friedrich Hebbel [*sic*] who said, "What you can become, you are already." And as someone very, very special reminded me, and as Henry Ford said, "One who fears limits his activities. Failure is only the opportunity to more intelligently begin again." I have been given an opportunity for a new beginning.

OTHER REAL PEOPLE

Looking at the learning patterns of real people may give crossover students a good sense of what others have experienced. We can look at the biographies of several well-known persons and find evidence of crossover traits.

Leonardo da Vinci used nearly undecipherable mirror writing. One biographer (Bramley, 1991) wrote, "Leonardo was left-handed. He could in fact write with both hands and in either direction . . . his shading is always from right to left, unlike that of right-handed artists . . . it did suit very well his taste for secrecy" (p.133).

Toksvig (1969) described the school experiences of Hans Christian Andersen in this way: "Hans Christian did not know his lessons especially well, but this was due, as it quite often is, to his being too clever. He learned by heart with astonishing facility . . . but he never learned to spell" (p. 18). According to another biographer (Godden, 1966), "He wrote poems, too, but spent most of his time dreaming or reading. He could not spell or write a clear sentence or do the smallest sum, but he devoured any book he could get hold of and learned whole pieces of them and scenes of plays by heart" (p. 27).

Vice-president Nelson Rockefeller struggled with reading and writing difficulties his entire life. Kramer and Roberts (1976) wrote, "When he was nine, Nelson was enrolled in the progressive Lincoln School in Manhattan, which could give personal attention to his tendency to transpose numbers and letters—a recurrent ailment called dyslexia which was aggravated by early attempts to 'cure' his left-handedness and later required him to memorize speeches to avoid stumbling over his own words" (p. 39). Kramer and Roberts (1976) quoted Rockefeller as saying, "I have never studied these things, but they say this has a psychological effect if you're left-handed and you're forced to, you know . . . and so you can't spell. I have a little trouble with reverse reading, too" (p. 39).

A number of modern celebrities have discussed their disabilities in various media. Actors Cher, Tom Cruise, Danny Glover, and Olympian Bruce Jenner are among those who have spoken out about their painful school experiences. It was interesting to observe the press accounts of John F. Kennedy, Jr.'s three attempts to pass the bar. At no time were his difficulties linked to earlier accounts of his reading disability. In a children's book about the Olympic diver Greg Louganis, Milton (1989) wrote, "And when the teacher called on him to read out loud he wished he could just disappear. . . . When he looked at a word, the letters seemed all mixed up. Sometimes he read words backwards. Sometimes the letters did not make any sense at all" (p.15).

If your experience includes interaction with either children with learning disabilities or those with gifts and/or talents, these brief descriptions hold phrases and behaviors familiar to you. Learning disabled/gifted (LD/G) children, whom I have chosen to call "crossover children," are a strange, fascinating amalgamation of those behaviors, those problems, and those joys that we associate with both learning disability and giftedness. Crossover children are bright! Engaging one of them in a conversation about an area of interest leaves no doubt about that fact. Crossover children have mild to serious learning problems. Looking at their report cards or listening to their teachers or parents underscores the very real educational concern they cause. Crossover children are frustrated. They sense the uneasiness caused by their unique intellectual abilities. They are often targets of such adult pronouncements as, "You could do better if you would only pay attention," or "How can someone who speaks so well write so poorly?"

Parents of crossover children are often at a loss to find help for their children. They have seen the giftedness in the preschool years or in the hobbies and interests of the child at home. From teachers, however, they hear about reading and writing problems or inability to sit still and pay attention. In spite of these concerns, crossover children may be doing average or above average work and may not qualify for school programs designed to help students with learning disabilities. If an intelligence test has been given that supports the observable superior intelligence, the likelihood that service will be available diminishes in some school districts. Many educators simply do not believe that a learning disability can exist in an otherwise gifted person! Paradoxically, high intelligence may increase the availability of service for others in districts where learning disability is determined by a discrepancy (testable difference) between ability and achievement. Low functioning in any of the basic skills may result in a discrepancy legally worthy of service.

Teachers of crossover children are concerned. They find that these children, at their very best, are full of enthusiasm, information, and eagerness to learn. They also find an inability to complete written assignments, some difficulty with reading, and a tendency to bog down in any task that requires sustained attention. How could anyone with such ability and promise have such problems?

This is the context in which crossover children live, learn, and grow. My personal interest in this group grew from hearing the concerns of both teachers and parents. Their stories were convincing evidence that these children were not rare, but that they constitute a sizable subpopulation of both the LD and gifted groups.

THE CROSSOVER PROFILE

Significant interest in gifted children with disabilities, including learning disability, began about 20 years ago (e.g., Maker, 1977; Whitmore, 1980). Since that time, the literature on crossover children has fallen into four categories: (a) case studies of individual children, (b) reports on pilot educational programs designed to serve this unique population, (c) studies of intellectual test patterns, most notably those associated with the Wechsler tests (1974, 1991) or of other specific psychological/learning traits, and (d) suggestions for teaching strategies appropriate for these children. Additionally, a better understanding of attention deficit/hyperactivity disorder (ADHD) (APA, 1994) and the overlapping symptoms of ADHD and giftedness (Webb & Latimer, 1993) has enhanced our knowledge about the apparent high energy levels, distractibility, and disorganization traits found in many crossover children. Using these resources and validating them through my own opportunity to study crossover children in a variety of contexts, I have developed a composite of the crossover child. (Appendix D contains an expanded reading list of primary sources.) Recognizing that no one child will fit the complete list, the composite consists of both gifted and LD characteristics:

Like other gifted children, the typical crossover child will:

- Intellectually approach or reach the gifted range (in this group, 120 IQ or above Full Scale IQ; 130 IQ or above in the strongest factor, Verbal Comprehension or Perceptual Organization using Wechsler scores).

- Have more interest and ability in pursuing broadbased, thematic topics than in remembering and dealing with details. ". . . the harder the task, the better they do; it's the easy work they can't master" (Silverman, 1989, p. 39).

- Be somewhat more of an intuitive "dreamer" than a practically oriented thinker; creativity or problem solving ability may be exhibited in a specific area of interest.

- Exhibit a sophisticated sense of humor.

- Visualize well and do well in areas requiring this ability (e.g., mathematics, especially geometry; art).

- Be highly sensitive and base decisions on personal feeling and human need rather than on logic as a young child, but may become more logical in adolescence.

- Have a high "readiness to learn" and a great interest in learning when topics are presented in a challenging manner.

Like children of average ability with learning disabilities, the typical crossover child will:

- Have an uneven intellectual pattern on the Wechsler intelligence tests with verbal comprehension and perceptual organization scores superior to those tapping attentional or sequencing abilities.

- Have an uneven academic pattern with strengths most likely in mathematics or content areas and weaknesses in the language arts areas—especially written language—but variations exist.

- Have written language difficulties including poor handwriting, poor mechanics, and difficulty in organizing content.

- Need remediation for skills deficits (but will respond better to teaching in context than to isolated skill building).

- Be distractible in large groups and have difficulty in completing work because of that distractibility.

- Have difficulty in organizing time and materials, often resulting in forgetting or incompletion of homework or in need of excessive time for completion.

- Need medical monitoring because he or she may benefit from medication and/or behavioral intervention for ADHD.

- Need more time to process language and respond than would be expected of someone with high intellectual capabilities.

- Lack some social skills and common sense decision making ability.

- Sometimes exhibit visual or auditory perceptual deficits or unusual visual sensitivity to light.

- Be less successful when confronted with input from multiple sources or with tasks that require the integration of multiple skills.

SUMMARY

A body of literature based on research studies and, to a greater extent, on clinical experience documents the critical characteristics of the learning disabled/gifted population. Crossover children may be more capable in either verbal or performance items on the Wechsler Intelligence Scale for Children-Revised Edition (WISC-R) or Wechsler Intelligence Scale for Children-Third Edition (WISC-III), but they tend to be significantly less able to perform at a superior level on those items tapping attentiveness, short-term memory, sequencing skills, and visual hyperacuity. They may initially be discovered because of their reading difficulties, but long-term academic problems more often lie in their inability to spell, write, and put down their thoughts in a cohesive written product. Crossover children vary from being extremely creative to exhibiting little creativity. Their learning styles reflect their giftedness and support the contention that they are capable thinkers but poor detail and organization people.

Finally, in spite of their ability to perform in the superior or gifted range on individual intelligence tests, their brains appear to function differently and less efficiently than nondisabled students of similar ability. These differences may manifest themselves in atypical visual or auditory functioning or inefficient processing of higher level cognitive tasks. Reaching full potential may rely upon receiving interventions such as learning cognitive strategies to overcome cognitive inefficiency, enriching the curriculum to support the self-concept of being gifted, and remediating the specific skill deficits that exist in each individual.

References

American Psychiatric Association (1994). *Diagnostic and statistical manual of mental disorders* (4th ed.). Washington, DC: Author.

Bramley, S. (1991). *Leonardo: Discovering the life of Leonardo da Vinci.* New York: Burlingame.

Godden, R. (1966). *Hans Christian Andersen: A great life in brief.* New York: Knopf.

Kramer, M., & Roberts, S. (1976). *"I never wanted to be vice-president of anything": An investigative biography of Nelson Rockefeller.* New York: Basic Books.

Maker, J. (1977). *Providing programs for the gifted handicapped.* Reston, VA: The Council for Exceptional Children.

Milton, J. (1989). *Greg Louganis: Diving for gold.* New York: Random House.

Silverman, L. (1989). Invisible gifts, invisible handicaps. *Roeper Review, 12,* 37–42.

Toksvig, S. (1969). *The life of Hans Christian Andersen.* New York: Harcourt, Brace.

Webb, J., & Latimer, D. (July, 1993). ADHD and children who are gifted. *ERIC Digest* (EDO-EC-93-5). Reston, VA: The Council for Exceptional Children.

Wechsler, D. (1974). *Wechsler Intelligence Scale for Children-Revised Edition.* Riverside, CA: The Psychological Corporation.

Wechsler, D. (1991). *Wechsler Intelligence Scale for Children- III.* San Antonio: The Psychological Corporation.

Whitmore, J. (1980). *Giftedness, conflict, and underachievement.* Boston: Allyn & Bacon.

2

Educational Planning and Programming

They wanted to give him an LD tutor an hour a day and put him in the gifted class a day a week! He can't get his regular classwork done now. We'd all be nervous wrecks!

He's a different kid when he's on the computer, but I have to be fair to all of the students. I have 23 of them and only two computers.

She made the Future Problem Solving team and they went all the way to the state competition. It's made all of the difference in the world in how she feels about herself. Now, she's making plans to go to gifted camp with some of those kids.

This book began with a discussion of the frustration faced by parents and professionals who must deal with a child who has such divergent strengths and weaknesses as those found in the crossover child. This chapter elaborates upon the same theme with some suggestions for action.

TIPS FOR PARENTS

One barrier that must be overcome is the tendency for parents and professionals to develop an adversarial relationship when faced with an unusual educational dilemma. Public education, for the most part, is an endeavor of good people trying to do good things while facing time, budget, and public support restraints. Good parenting, for the most part, includes wanting and being willing to fight for the best possible education for each of our children. In the case of an atypical child, educational reality and parental wishes may conflict.

School programs are usually provided for groups of children with similar needs. Unless it is a large system, the likelihood of having 10 to 15 crossover children of similar ages and needs in a single school system is not great. Given this fact, appropriate educational plans that do not include a "crossover class" need to be developed. Parents should understand that several factors hinder this planning process.

One such hindrance is that the true nature of the child's ability or disability may not be understood. Because of discrepant abilities or ADHD tendencies, the main focus may be on the behavior problems of crossover children. Or if, in spite of disabilities, crossover children are able to perform at average or above average rates, they may be considered erratic or lazy children who sometimes do well but often resist doing good work. Parents may have better instincts about their child's real ability in such cases than do the professionals, but may find themselves at a loss to explain the paradoxical behavior. At such times, parents need to insist on a complete evaluation of the child, keep close home/school communication, and educate themselves about the problem.

Another hindrance is that educators may lack needed information about the typical characteristics of students with learning disabilities and those who are gifted. Very few will have knowledge of the interaction of LD and giftedness. Universities are making inroads in educating general education teachers in this area, but teachers who attended college some time ago may not have had this training. A parent who can speak with some authority on the subject, firmly and with controlled emotionality, is more likely to encourage professional support than one who speaks from the heart, but with limited information. (Appendixes A and B list sources of information for both parents and professionals.)

A third hindrance is that, given all of their responsibilities, school administrators may not see the need for atypical programming for a single crossover child. One tactic that seems helpful in approaching school personnel is for parents to band together in support or informational groups. While confidentiality prohibits sharing names of children with specific needs, becoming room volunteers or PTA members may bring concerned parents into contact with one another. Other resources or existing groups may be found by contacting regional special education centers or state departments of education. In some areas, support groups are listed in telephone directories. A single family requesting special services can be put off, but a persistent group can, over time, have success. One of the difficult parts of parent advocacy is that those who start movements often see programs develop too late to help their own children. Those who benefit do not appreciate the struggle of their predecessors and, therefore, lack the fervor it takes to perpetuate the existence of such groups. Support groups that survive over time seem to have leaders who commit to the cause as well as to the specific needs of their own children.

Finally, both teachers and parents must adopt the attitude that it should be the parent and teacher against the problem, not against each other or the child. Overcoming a frustration-based adversarial position is a major need before adequate programming can be started. Some ideas for parents include the following:[1]

- *Make a list of specific observations or questions before each conference.* It is harder to get lost in emotional tangents with a script in hand.

- *Assume that your child's teacher cares about children and about your child specifically.* If the teacher's behavior contradicts this, assume that he or she is working from an inadequate information base about your child and about the interaction of learning disability and giftedness. Find a kind way to supply the teacher with information and resources. (For example, take in an article and say, "I found this really helpful with Johnny at home. I thought you might want to read it, too.")

- *Do not hesitate to request the involvement of school personnel beyond the classroom teacher.* The principal, school counselor, and school psychologist all have a responsibility to consult with parents and teachers on such matters. The most helpful

---

[1] I am indebted to Dr. Marsha Schubert for several of these suggestions.

person in your school may vary, so get to know each of them. Parents sometimes go to outside consultants before they search within the school district. Ultimately, the problem must be solved within the school, and it is here that the search for assistance should start.

- *Set priorities.* When necessary, share those priorities with your child's teachers. Is having a "B" average worth 4 or 5 hours of homework every night and/or giving up extracurricular activities? It is important to set realistic goals and demands for both parents and the child. How much stress can everyone tolerate? It is important to spend time together in family and recreational activities as well as in academically focused work sessions.

- *Set aside time each night to help your child organize and plan work.* This ability is lacking in many crossover children, and much time can be wasted without repeated supervision of the planning process. Sometimes, long homework sessions can be avoided through taking time to go through this step. The next chapter elaborates upon specific methods of organizing such as using an assignment notebook, planning several days in advance, and color coding by subject or project.

- *Do not hesitate to ask for specific teachers for your child.* This can be an administrative nightmare, and your request may not be accommodated. Most crossover children do better with teachers who provide a structured environment but will tolerate the child's inability to live within that structure all of the time. Since these are the best teachers for most children, they may be in high demand. Expect to win a few and lose a few requests. If your child is assigned to a rigid teacher with high expectations, help the teacher understand why your child will not meet these expectations consistently, but express support for the structure he or she can provide. If the teacher is less organized but more cognizant of the emotional and creative needs of your child, support this strength but stress the need for firmness and structure in your child's environment and underscore the child's difficulty in providing it independently.

- *Look for a support group or consider starting one if none exists.* Existing groups will most likely focus on either giftedness or learning disability. It may be necessary to join both and/or request discussions and programs about the crossover condition.

- *Do not expect overnight miracles.* Some time may pass before you, your child, and his teachers learn to live with the child's unique needs. If your child falls behind because no professional remedial help is available, look for alternatives. Parents seldom make good tutors because emotionality quickly overrules rationality. Peer or cross-age tutors may be available in the school. The latter may be preferable because it is easier to display one's weaknesses to another student who is not a classmate. Even better, make the crossover child a tutor for a younger child. This is most helpful when the tutor has previously studied with the tutee's current teacher. Both benefit because an ideal way to reinforce basic skill learning is to teach it to someone else.

  Out-of-school volunteers or private tutors may be other sources of assistance. Those who can provide or understand the assessment information about a child and will use it to determine the teaching/learning needs are preferable to those who have "canned" remedial programs. The latter may focus on a narrow set of skills such as phonics that may or may not match your child's needs. Remember, the evidence is overwhelming that crossover children learn basic skills best when the skills are presented within the context of meaningful content.

- *Seek out community enrichment activities.* If the bulk of interactions emphasize the child's disabilities, look for Saturday, evening, or summer programs that support the child's ability. Local museums, libraries, universities, summer recreation programs, and camps offer experiences that will provide such suppport. Entrance and class requirements of summer school classes may be more flexible than for classes taught during the regular school year. A crossover child who is denied entrance into a gifted resource program during the academic year may be allowed to participate in summer activities with other gifted children. Parents need to control the time spent in such activities during the academic year, but permission to participate should never depend on getting good grades. Access to an activity that enhances one's ability should not depend on overcoming one's disability. Both need to be accommodated at the same time.

- *Listen carefully to what your child is or is not saying.* Verbal and nonverbal signs of anxiety and stress should be addressed quickly and, if necessary, collaboratively with educators or outside professionals. Crossover children know what they cannot do successfully. In many ways, good basic intelligence makes this understanding keener and the pain deeper.

- *Practice self-restraint.* Do not do everything for your child or take over responsibilities that rightfully belong to him or her. It is natural to try to protect a child from a seemingly rigid and uncaring world, but "learned helplessness" can be a greater hindrance to lifelong success and happiness than a specific academic deficiency . Support, don't "do for," your child.

TIPS FOR EDUCATORS

School personnel can support parents by encouraging some of the experiences just mentioned or accepting suggestions from parents that are feasible and educationally sound. Additionally, there are techniques that will facilitate home/school communication.

- *If parental frustration targets you, understand it for what it is and do not take it personally.* On the other hand, if parents have read on the subject and offer you information you do not already have, accept it graciously. Do not negate the layperson who has gathered information before you. Accepting the parent as a team equal will enhance the communication process.

- *Get a support team involved quickly.* Few of us have enough skill and information to go it alone. If your school has a Teacher Assistance Team (TAT), involve them in planning for your child. The TAT is a group of educators who meet periodically to consult with teachers within their buildings on the problems of specific children. A consultation, problem-solving model is used rather than an expert approach, such as turning the child over to a school psychologist for "fixing" or bringing in an outside consultant. The purpose of the TAT is to provide support from peers, to expand the teaching repertoire of the participants to better meet the needs of atypical children, and to help determine whether or not additional support personnel should be involved in assisting the child in question (see Chalfant & Pysh, 1979). Even though the child may remain in the regular classroom, input from both the LD and gifted education teacher or consultant could be invaluable.

- *If the crossover child is a preteen or adolescent, understand his or her particular vulnerability.* Being one of the gang is jeopardized by both the disability and the ability. Individuals or groups of students looking for their own identities may accept a student excluded by mainstream groups within the school. If this is observed either at school or at home, a concerted effort should be made to provide positive alternative activities. Teachers who advise clubs or other extracurricular activities may wish to invite the crossover child to join. It may also be helpful to provide service or leadership opportunities whenever possible. The child who can see and serve the needs of others is less likely to remain overly focused on his or her own problems.

- *Take signs of depression seriously.* The typical ups and downs of adolescent emotionality may be magnified in a teenager with special needs. Some signs of depression are unusual eating habits, unusual sleep patterns, low energy, low self-esteem, poor concentration, or feelings of hopelessness (American Psychiatric Association, 1994). If these seem to characterize the adolescent (or child) most of the time, seek help. Waiting it out may lead to serious consequences.

- *Involve yourself or provide other mentors.* The crossover child needs positive adult role models. An effective way to provide role models is to involve the child in a mentoring project. A mentor is usually a community volunteer who shares an avocational interest or whose vocation represents a potential career goal of the mentee. A mentor should be aware of the particular needs of the child and should be given some assistance in relating to any unusual behavior such as attentional difficulty. By focusing on a shared interest, relationships can take on dimensions different from those the child has developed with parents, teachers, or peers.

- *Be flexible and encourage flexibility in your colleagues.* The crossover child is an ideal candidate for the "but we've never done it this way before" cop-out. The cornerstone concept of American education is that every child deserves an equal opportunity to perform well. The rarity of the crossover condition may necessitate breaking new ground within a school system and within individual classrooms.

PROGRAMMING FOR THE CROSSOVER CHILD

One of the most difficult decisions to make is where to place the crossover child in school while delivering the available services. Some children may learn to compensate for their disability to the degree that they are ineligible for LD services but are overlooked for gifted programs. Others will qualify for both LD and gifted programs and could benefit from both. Unfortunately, participation in both special programs and the regular class can provide a disjointed experience for a child who needs structure and organization as much as curricular content. An inclusion model in which the child stays in the regular classroom and receives support from specialists may work for many, but there seems to be no one solution for every crossover child's dilemma. Joint decision making involving parents and all of the program specialists is imperative.

Some questions that may assist in the decision-making process are these:

- Is the child *learning* basic skills but not *completing* work, or truly deficient in the skills themselves? Learning skills may require remediation; completion of work may require teaching organization or controlling ADHD.

- Has medical assistance been sought to control any ADHD problems?

- Can the child control the ADHD characteristics when additional structure is provided (such as a carrel)?

- Does the child exhibit giftedness in class discussions or in topics of particular interest?

- Does the child share creative ideas, produce art work, or exhibit unusual talent in one of the performing arts?

- Is the child's self-concept one of ability, disability, or a realistic combination of both? Is there a need to provide social skills instruction and self-esteem building?

- Are the teachers who may be involved in the child's placement willing to accommodate any special needs, and are they open to being educated more fully about ways to help such a child?

- Which teachers use or are willing to use a combination of clinical and holistic teaching methods (as described in Chapter 4)?

- If the disability is academic, is it considered a long-term problem or could an intensive, short-term intervention provide the needed assistance?

- How flexible are the teachers in permitting the use of and how available are compensatory devices such as computers or calculators?

The ideal answer to each of these questions may be obvious, but the reality will vary greatly from school to school. A plan for using the best resources a particular school can offer should be put into place. These are priority steps for implementing such a plan.

- *If medical intervention is needed, it should be sought early and maintained as long as necessary.* If medication is part of the treatment plan, continuous monitoring by a physician is necessary to ensure proper dosage and desired results.

- *Structure and organization skills that help one to keep track of external belongings and develop internal thought processes should be the first basic skills to be taught.* Remembering assignments, getting books and homework from school to home and back, managing time to allow for recreation as well as study, and generally holding one's life together are major obstacles for most crossover and LD children. They need direct instruction in developing these skills that are important components of successful achievement in all academic areas.

- *Remediation should be considered until a functional reading and mathematics repertoire is in place.* Comprehension during silent reading, not perfect word-for-word oral reading ability, should be the goal. Depending upon the severity of the skill deficit(s), a variety of delivery systems may be used. Differentiated teaching within the regular classroom, professional or supervised cross-age tutors, or partial attendance in an LD resource room or remedial reading program are some possibilities. Individual school systems may have other choices available.

- *If basic reading and math skills are in place but written assignments are not completed adequately, placement in a gifted program may be considered if both the gifted and general education teacher(s) are willing to accept word processed papers or nonwritten products for some assignments.* Again, a variety of options other than the gifted resource room may provide more appropriate service for some children. Differentiating curriculum and assignments within the general classroom, intermittent contact with a gifted consultant (for either the child or the regular class teacher), independent study contracts (once basic research skills have been learned), mentorships or cross-age partnerships, and extracurricular tournaments or projects may better fit the available time and specific skills of some crossover children. Regardless of the option chosen, compacting or testing out of some regular class work will be necessary to keep the daily workload manageable.

- *If the decision is to provide LD services but not gifted programming, support services should provide reinforcement of the child's giftedness in spite of the disability.* If inclusionary services are provided in a school district, support for both the LD and gifted needs may be available in the regular classroom. If not, depending upon the skills of the people involved, assistance could be provided by the regular class teacher, the LD teacher, a school counselor, or a school psychologist. Ideally, all would support the goal of fostering self-esteem. If the school personnel cannot provide such a service, outside help should be sought. Ultimately, it is the child's sense of self-worth more than academic ability that will determine the ability to cope in the adult world.

- *Regardless of the placement, an early emphasis should be placed on the necessity and appropriateness of using compensatory technology such as word processing, spell checks, and calculators.* As adults, many of us use these devices freely, almost exclusively, to complete our daily tasks. Appropriate use of these devices should be taught to all children at an early age, and it should be considered mandatory for the crossover group. The rapid movement toward including technology in the classroom makes this goal more feasible with every passing year.

- *Regardless of the placement, frequent input from all concerned specialists should be sought.* The LD teacher and the gifted educator should consult regularly. Ideas and concerns of the regular class teacher, input on the affective needs of the child from the school counselor or psychologist, and the parent's viewpoints must also be shared on a regular basis. The trend toward collaboration and inclusion in special education has made this type of communication common in many districts where it was once a rarity and difficult to achieve.

- *As the child enters the upper grades, some specific planning must take place.* Possible career goals have to be explored against the backdrop of residual disability. For instance, working in engineering or business might be an unrealistic career goal for a student with a math disability. Reality checks through "shadowing" professionals and checking out college courses of study need to be completed prior to enrolling in high school academic tracks. If college is a goal, the crossover child should be encouraged to enroll in college preparatory courses, but counselors must be alerted to the child's particular needs. Support services should be maintained throughout all grades as needed.

- *The crossover child should be encouraged to become involved in extracurricular academic activities that fit his or her particular gifts.* Such competitions as *Odyssey of the Mind* or *Future Problem Solving* may highlight the skills of the child who will never be a spelling bee champion or do exceptionally well on standardized tests. Gifted educators should have specific information about the variety of options available in a local community.

- *The child should be involved in the decision making process as soon as it is practical.* Adults often huddle around discussing the fate of children without sharing their thoughts with or soliciting the input of the child in question. One of the highest goals of life is to control one's own destiny. Self-advocacy is an essential lifelong skill that can be taught, in part, through careful inclusion of the child in meetings concerning him or her. By discussing the plusses, minuses, and interesting features (PMI) of each educational option, the child, parents, and educators can better reach the best solution among the realistic options available.

SUMMARY

Crossover children can be difficult but delightful puzzles. Given the proper support, they can succeed, prosper, contribute, and maintain a sense of self-worth in spite of the obstacles they will face. The tools for success are available. Understanding and educating learning disabled/gifted children can be accomplished by those who care enough to meet the challenge.

16

References

American Psychiatric Association (1994). *Diagnostic and statistical manual of mental disorders* (4th ed.). Washington, DC: Author

Chalfant, J., & Pysh, M. (1979). Teacher Assistance Teams: A model for within-building problem solving. *Learning Disability Quarterly, 2,* 85-96.

3

Behavioral and Social Interventions

She knew every spelling word before she went to bed, but she got a 68 on the test.

He and his parents insist that he finishes his homework every night, but I can't give credit for what I never see!

I insist that Mickey clean his desk and take home papers every Friday. By Tuesday, it looks as if a tornado has been hired as the housekeeper!

She never turns in big papers on time. She tells me that she wants to get it "just right" before she gives it to me.

Four common and troublesome characteristics of students with learning disabilities are impulsivity, disorganization, distractibility, and poor memory. These traits may interfere with compliance with behavioral expectations, with completing work and/or getting it in on time, and with learning assigned material, especially isolated information such as spelling words and basic mathematics facts. These are legitimate concerns that must be addressed if a child is to be a successful student. When these problems occur, educators are reluctant to consider gifted programming even if a crossover child qualifies on the basis of test scores and demonstrates high potential in some areas.

Students with learning disabilities as well as those who are gifted may have difficulty maintaining a sense of balance and emotional well-being when faced with being different from the majority of their peers. Both groups may have rather severe social problems. Gifted students may be most affected by their shyness and introversion. Further, they may experience a sense of isolation and alienation from their peers. A social skills deficit is one of the ways in which a student's learning disability may be manifested. As usual, the crossover child may face either or both sets of problems.

CONTROLLING IMPULSIVITY

The tendency to jump into a situation without thinking or making a plan of attack characterizes the impulsive child. This behavior is evident in approaching academic work and everyday life. Helping the child control impulsivity may require consistent and concerted effort from everyone concerned. Walking through (modeling) rather than talking through (verbal) control techniques should be used. Initial instruction may need to focus on specific situations. A description of two programs that are based on cognitive behavioral modification (CBM) follows, as does a scenario for attacking one child's unique problems.

Meichenbaum's Cognitive-Behavioral Modification and *Think Aloud*

Psychologist Donald Meichenbaum has developed procedures designed to assist impulsive children in controlling their own behavior. His work focuses on the seemingly diminished ability of such children to verbally mediate (control with self-talk) impulses that more reflective children mediate and control with little effort. In some of his early work, Meichenbaum (1977) observed two groups of preschool children who were characterized as either impulsive or reflective. The former used immature language primarily for self-stimulation, while the latter used language for communicating with others or for self-control. Out of this and similar research, he concluded that impulsive children may appear impulsive because they do not understand the requirements of a task, because they do not use self-talk for self-control, or because they produce self-talk but fail to heed their own words.

Meichenbaum developed a direct instructional procedure to help impulsive children develop more efficient use of their self-regulatory behavior. Simply, it assists children to "Stop! Look! and Listen!" before acting. The steps used to teach a child these self-control techniques are as follows:

1. The adult model performs a task while thinking out loud about what he or she should do. For example, " When I do two-column addition, I need to line my columns up straight, start adding in the ones' column and be sure to carry from the ones' to the tens' column." (Cognitive modeling.)
2. The child performs the same task under the direction of the model following the model's words while doing the problem. (Direct, overt guidance.)
3. The child performs the task while instructing himself out loud. (Overt self-guidance)
4. The child whispers instruction to himself while doing the task. (Faded self-guidance)
5. The child does the task while using private speech. (Covert self-guidance).

(Meichenbaum, 1977, pp. 32–33.

The initial tasks used by Meichenbaum were simple sensorimotor tasks such as copying, coloring within the lines, and solving puzzles. Later, Camp and Bash (1985) developed a complete instructional program for elementary school children under the title *Think Aloud.* Their introduction to the three workbooks (for grades 1–2, 3–4, and 5–6) and teacher's manuals suggest that their program can be used in regular classrooms and that groups of 10 children are the ideal. Their manual provides specific instructions for the teacher's dialogue with the students as well as worksheets that can be duplicated. Lessons include those which emphasize such skills as labeling, sequencing, and categorizing; but most identify and solve problems with emotional content.

Posters of the major cuing device, a bear or a dragon, are to be placed in the room. The posters remind the children of the following sequence: "What am I supposed to do?"; "What are some plans?"; "How is my plan working?"; and "How did I do?" (Camp & Bash, 1985, pp. 49–51).

Kendall's *Stop and Think*

Closely akin to *Think Aloud* is the work of Phillip Kendall that has as its focus the control of impulsivity and anxiety through the use of common academic content. The five-step problem solving process taught to the children includes a "Focus in" step, but otherwise parallels the steps of Bush and Camp. Since variations on creative problem solving are found in literature on both learning disability and giftedness, this should be a familiar and favorite strategy regardless of the setting. Kendall's (1988) specific sequence is as follows:

1. "What am I supposed to do?" or "What is the problem?"
2. "Look at all of the possibilities" (Generate alternatives)
3. "Focus in" (Try to shut out environmental and mental distractions)
4. "Pick an answer" (Choose from among the alternatives)
5. "Check out my answer" and "Praise myself if I'm right and, if not, try to go more slowly and work more carefully next time." (pp. 2–3)

The *Stop and Think* workbook provides practice in such basic skills as sequencing, shape differentiation, simple mathematics, opposites, word searches, and describing emotions connected to various facial expressions. This variety of content underscores the universality of the problem-solving approach. The "focus in" step is an excellent addition for the distractible or impulsive student.

Behavioral Strategies

While cognitive behavioral strategies are preferable because of their self-control aspects, some younger or highly impulsive children may lack the self-talk ability to implement them. In these cases, traditional behavioral modification techniques may be used to start the process. A few examples of impulse controllers include the development of a reward system for improvement of specific problems such as not completing work, blurting out, shoving, or getting out of line. Charting behavior, setting timers for intermittent reinforcement, or having children keep their own charts are well-established procedures. It is assumed that most readers are acquainted with behavioral approaches. If not, resources that describe the fundamentals are available at any professional library.

Personalizing Behavior Management

Let us assume that Ed, a second grader, has been having difficulty at school because of his impulsive behavior. The specific behaviors have been identified as speaking out of turn in class, hitting back on the playground at the slightest provocation, and going beyond the playground limits into neighboring yards. Each can be treated as a separate behavior, and it is important that they not be grouped into a "bad boy" generalization.

In the case of speaking out of turn, a combination of a self-talk script and visual reminder might be used to help Ed gain control over this behavior. The script, which can be written by Ed and a teacher or counselor, might include the following sequence:

1. *What am I supposed to do?*

   The class rule is no talking without raising my hand.

2. *What are some plans?*

   When I know the answer I should raise my hand.

   When I want to talk out I should touch my signal. It will help me to raise my hand.

3. *Focus in*

   This is discussion time. I must remember my signal and what it means.

4. *How is my plan working?*

   I will keep a chart of each time I touch my signal instead of talking out.

   I will talk with my teacher once a day about my progress.

5. *How did I do?*

   My teacher and I will look at my charts at the end of each week.

Signals can be such things as a rubber band on the wrist, a sticker on the hand, or a painted fingernail. For older children, a designated but unmarked part of the body should suffice. The self-talk sequence can be related to this signal through the counselor's teaching. A counselor might say, while touching the signal himself or herself, "This sticker is your 'don't talk' signal. When it is touched, you will remember to raise your hand before talking." Through repeated practice, the child should be able to activate the signal independently.

CONTROLLING DISORGANIZATION

One can spot the disorganized child with very little training. Papers abound on top of and inside the child's desk and usually are falling out along with books and other belongings. Notebooks are stuffed with a hodge-podge of returned work and personal items. Getting homework to and from home is a major endeavor. Lunches or lunch money and permissions for field trips frequently require frantic phone calls home. This inability to organize the simplest of tasks plagues many children with disabilities, their families, and their teachers. Preaching, scolding, or punishing has little effect on solving this problem. Whatever internal mechanism develops in most of us that allows us to live with some sense of order is deficient in these children. Externally imposed controls must be set up and monitored. Eventually, the disorganized child must accept the need for artificial organizers. Significant adults must accept that it is necessary to provide them way beyond the time when "he should be responsible for doing these things by himself."

The behavior of the parent is critical in controlling disorganization. If parents have the same tendency, they must understand that, to help their child, they may have to adjust their own lifestyles to include more orderly approaches to daily schedules, mealtimes, or planning ahead for family outings. Family lifestyle will not cause disorganization in the child with learning disabilities, but it can enhance or impede the child's ability to control impulsive behavior. Similarly, a disordered classroom will not provide a good model for such a child. Conversely, a rigid sense of order may place the child in a situation he or she is incapable of responding to, and serious teacher/child conflicts may result. The following are some specific organizers that may help disorganized children:

- *Use color coding.* This may be used in notebooks that have color-differentiated sections for each subject, on closet shelves that are matched by colored tape to the items that should be stored there, or by tags sewn in clothing to indicate what shirt or pair of socks goes with which pair of pants. In the beginning, adult monitoring may be needed; but once routinized, color can help provide a simple structure to a potentially chaotic environment.

- *Set up repetitious routines for daily activities.* Homework *always* should be done at the desk, then placed by the front door in the evening, so that the frantic morning search can be avoided. Clothes for the next day *always* should be selected before going to bed so that matching socks are assured for 7 a.m. Well, you get the idea! Nothing should be left to chance *or* mornings!

- *Carry small notebooks for recording assignments.* If teachers and parents need to check for accuracy and completeness, a simple initialling by both parents and teacher can serve as an adult communication scheme.

- *Write out a complete daily schedule each evening before going to bed.* Building on paper a life that includes classes, study time, and recreation helps the child ensure that all of this will occur with predictability and balance.

You may be able to devise other schemes for providing the structure needed by the disorganized child. As adults, our responsibility is to set up the structure, monitor it, and reinforce it until it becomes routinized. Expect errors, excuses, and backsliding; but help the child to make steady progress though consistent, supportive reminders.

INCREASING ATTENTION

Many children with learning disabilities, including crossover children, are unable to sustain attention appropriately. Simon (1986) explained that attention has three major roles in the learning process: (1) It allows us to focus on a particular problem for an extended period; (2) it helps us retrieve inactive memory elements when they are needed for current problem solving; and (3) it allows us to shift the focus and content of our attention when it is required (e.g., to stop reading and answer a ringing telephone). The inability to maintain sufficient control over these three attentional processes is the essence of attention deficit.

Psychologists and psychiatrists use the Diagnostic and Statistical Manual of the American Psychiatric Association to differentiate among different troublesome or pathological behavioral conditions. The most current manual (the *DSM-IV*, American Psychiatric Association, 1994) lists the following characteristics of ADHD. Children may be diagnosed as inattentive, as hyperactive-impulsive, or as a combination of both. Children must exhibit six or more of the criteria for more than a 6-month period and "to a degree that is maladaptive and inconsistent with developmental level" (p. 83). The following symptoms are a simplification of the criteria listed in the DSM-IV (pp. 83–84):

Inattentiveness (Exhibits six or more)

- Failure to pay close attention to details; careless mistakes in schoolwork.
- Difficulty sustaining attention while working or playing.
- Does not listen even when spoken to directly.
- Does not follow instructions or complete assigned tasks.
- Has difficulty organizing tasks and activities.
- Avoids or dislikes tasks requiring sustained mental effort.
- Often loses materials and books.
- Is easily distracted by extraneous stimuli (secondary sights, sounds, etc.).
- Is often forgetful in daily activities.

The impulsive-hyperactive child exhibits six or more of these symptoms:

Hyperactivity

- Fidgets with hands or feet or squirms in seat.
- May leave seat in classroom when it is inappropriate.
- May run or climb excessively or in inappropriate situations (or in adolescents and adults, have feelings of restlessness).
- May have difficulty in playing quietly.
- Is often "on the go."
- Often talks excessively.

Impulsivity

- Blurts out answers before questions have been completed.
- Has difficulty awaiting turn.
- Interrupts or intrudes on others.

The ability to control these behaviors depends upon the integrated functioning of many parts of the brain. Increased ability to integrate and control depends upon many factors including development (simply getting older), direct instruction in controlling the behavior (usually with the help of teachers, psychologists and/or parents), or medication. The medication commonly used to control ADHD (e.g., Ritalin and Cylert) biochemically increases the efficiency of the system at the point of nerve interface in about 70% to 80% of children for whom it is prescribed. This increased efficiency can pave the path for retraining by decreasing the ADHD behavior, but it has no direct effect on the learning disability (Silver, 1992). In less severe instances, development and instruction may provide enough support to bypass medication altogether. The difficult decision of whether or not to use medication should be made by the family in cooperation with a physician who is knowledgeable about ADHD and has good behavioral information from educators and parents about the child's functioning. Two books that provide excellent information about ADHD are *The Misunderstood Child: A Guide for Parents of Children with Learning Disabilities (2nd ed.)* (Silver, 1992) and *Driven to Distraction* (Hallowell & Ratey, 1994). The former has a particularly helpful discussion of medications and the issues that surround them; the latter provides numerous helpful hints for controlling ADHD in both children and adults.

An interesting sidebar to the prevalence of ADHD in today's children is the concern of some gifted educators that the high intensities, daydreaming, lack of persistence on low level tasks, questioning of rules and tradition, and low sleep needs of gifted children may be mistaken for attention deficit (Webb & Latimer, 1993). Webb and Latimer suggest that differential diagnosis can be accomplished by considering the setting and the situation: How pervasive is the behavior? Does it occur primarily in settings where the child is unchallenged? Does the child consistently achieve well with the possible exception of repetitive drill-and-practice work?) The best advice is to remember that learning disability, giftedness, and ADHD can exist separately or in any combination. Care should be taken to recognize the existence of any of the possible components, especially in crossover children.

Classroom Interventions

One has only to observe a child with ADHD for a few minutes in a classroom before it becomes obvious that the setting makes it difficult for the child to stay on task. Think of the distractions caused by the movement and noise of the other children; the teacher's presence and voice; and the bulletin boards, learning centers, and teaching materials common to most classrooms. While the nondistractible child may find these conditions comfortable and workable, most children with ADHD simply move from one distraction to another (often with both mind and body) at the expense of completing their daily work. It is no wonder that this is a major, perhaps primary, complaint about these children. The logical way to control too much stimulation is to eliminate or hide distracting factors. Classrooms for children with learning disabilities have used carrels or individual workplaces for decades. They are less prevalent in regular and gifted classrooms, often because teachers in these situations seem to equate them with punishment. Insisting that the distractible child work in a large group setting is a far greater punishment!

When the use of the "office" is handled appropriately, it can become rewarding rather than punishing. Teachers who work with distractible children in a positive way can teach them that they are the ones who can best decide when a sheltered workplace is needed. A secret signal between teacher and child can be used if the teacher observes that the child should consider moving to the carrel. Such a signal might be a Carol Burnett tug on the ear when the teacher is across the room or a touch on the shoulder when nearby. In any case, the development of an "It's our secret way to help you" system will reinforce the positive aspects of the experience rather than "You must go to the office because you're bothering others and not doing your own work." You and I against the problem is a much stronger position for positive change than the adversarial you against me.

Other problems arise when inattention is coupled with hyperactivity. Hyperactive children *have* to move. They may be confined to their seats by strict supervision or punishment; but they will move their feet, tap their pencils or toes, or find their own unique outlet for their need. A far better option when this urge becomes strong is to allow the child to walk to a designated spot, stretch to "get the kinks out," and return to working at his or her seat. This "movement" corner can be a small space designated by a piece of carpet or by tape on the floor. The rules might include no talking, one person at a time, a maximum stay of 3 minutes (measured by a noiseless hourglass egg timer), and a maximum number of visits per period or day depending upon the age and need of the child. Stopping for group stretch breaks will counteract motor and mental fatigue and will raise the work efficiency of all children. They should be part of the daily routine of every classroom.

If the child is older and these ideas would cause embarrassment, it may be necessary to work out private contracts between teacher and student to accommodate the child's needs without disrupting the classroom. For instance, the teacher may get a "pencil tapper" to wiggle toes or fingers noiselessly. Momentary inattention may be tolerated without teacher comment. If it is prolonged, the teacher may walk to the child and, with a shoulder tap, bring the child back to attention without any verbal interchange. Just *knowing* that the teacher *understands* may be the most powerful weapon of all.

ENHANCING MEMORY

An inability to remember information that has been taught and seemingly learned is a common descriptor of the crossover child or the child with learning disability. Consequently, the study of memory, or the storage and retrieval of information, is an area of considerable interest. Memory appears to have three components: short-term memory (STM), long-term memory (LTM), and working memory. Short-term memory lasts only 20 to 30 seconds and is the ability to deal with the information at hand. Long-term memory begins after the first half-second of attention. Even though information must pass through STM to be stored in LTM, both are occurring at the same time. Meaningful drill and practice will strengthen LTM (MacInnes & Robbins, 1987). Working memory is composed of an executive or control function, a verbal memory and storage loop, and an imagery and spatial memory "scratch-pad" (Baddeley, 1986). In this model, STM differs from working memory in that working memory not only stores new information, but also actively integrates the new information with old information that has been stored in long-term memory. The most efficient working memory is that in which the verbal, spatial, and control functions are working smoothly as a team. When too much information is presented, the overload that results must be stored using the control function. This, in turn, decreases the ability of the working memory to make sense out of the information (Swanson, Cochran, & Ewers, 1990).

A good example of the tendency for children with reading disabilities to overload the working memory capacity is their slow recognition of sequences of letters or words. If this capacity is tied up in slowly identifying words (e.g., in the laborious sounding-out process often observed in poor readers), little is left for comprehending those words or the meaning of the sentences and paragraphs of which they are a part (Das & Varnhagen, 1986).

Another example of the inter-relationship of the memory systems is the common problem of children with learning disabilities who can recite spelling words at home perfectly (relying primarily on STM), but then meet with limited success the next day at school (LTM). The home study fails to translate directly to school success. It might be suggested that if those words were studied in context (e.g.,in sentences) and in the same modality (e.g., written instead of oral practice), this additional meaning and structure would result in greater retention. The latter process would rely more on working memory than on STM because it would entail combining the new information (the spelling word) with the contextual information brought up from previously stored material.

A distinction made by Squire (1986) that is meaningful to educators is the difference between the memory for knowledge of skills and procedures (how to do it) and the memory for fact and episodes (school-like learning and the individual happenings in one's life). Persons with amnesia may retain the former but forget the latter, leading Squire to deduce that different systems are involved. Since the former are considered process (how to do it) skills and the latter are content (what to learn), they must be integrated for efficient learning. Crossover students often see the process relationships but cannot retrieve the individual facts needed to complete the problems or tasks. Students of more average ability who have learning disabilities may have difficulty with both process and content.

Memory deficits may be caused by a number of factors, but inappropriate storage will most certainly deter effective retrieval of the information needed to complete daily work. Cohen, Eysenck, and LeVoi (1986) cited the following ways in which the storage and retrieval process is enhanced:

- *Memory is enhanced when new information is meaningfully related with old.* For instance, relating "chair" to "desk" results in better long-term recall than relating "chair" to "hair," which rhymes and shares letter similarities. In teaching, beginning a lesson by reviewing the previously discussed information on that topic will help students "bring up" old learning and attach it to the new.

- *Memory is enhanced when it involves emotion or personal meaning.* Dramatic instances of this are "flashbulb" events such as vividly recalling where you were and what you were doing on the day of the Kennedy assassination, the beginning of the Gulf War, or a personal event such as the death of a loved one or a marriage proposal. Basing lessons upon personal content such as journals, creative writing, or favorite literature may be more appropriate resources than basal texts or spelling workbooks even when memory of isolated words or facts is desired.

- *Memory is enhanced when meaningful clues are provided to facilitate recall.* Multiple-choice tests are easier than essay tests in this regard, but some students may find that the holistic responses required by essay questions provide a structure that evokes a better-integrated response. Trying to relate verbal knowledge to sights or sounds or other sensory experience may solidify memory of the information.

- *All memory is stored in relation to and filtered through previously stored events.* Just as eyewitnesses at an accident do, we all "see" knowledge and new experiences in light of our individual pasts. Ausubel (1968) used the word *scaffolding* to explain this concept of relating old ideas and new ones and contended that it is an efficient way to both learn and retain new knowledge. For students who have experienced very little of the world, providing opportunities for field trips, speakers, and other real-life contacts may be necessary to enhance the required book learning of the classroom.

The cognitive strategies sequences described in this chapter and Chapter 4 provide a number of memory cues that correspond to this list, including associating new information with old, using analogies and metaphors to personalize and enhance meaning, and providing guided practice and generalization activities. Teachers who follow those sequences will assist children with memory deficiencies to integrate new learning with old in a much more methodical way than can be accomplished with the presentation of the same information in multiple unrelated worksheets.

Specific Memory Aids

Teaching groups of children limits an instructor's ability to attend to the needs of each individual child. The following good teaching practices should increase the likelihood of learning in children with both attentional and memory deficits, despite the group setting.

- *Use learning "set" procedures to cue children that something important will be said.* For example, start a lesson by saying, " This is a new idea that I am going to share with you. Remember that yesterday we talked about the causes of the Civil War? Today we are going to continue that discussion, but first, can anyone tell me one important thing we learned about this topic yesterday?" This phrasing will signal the need for attention, a precursor for both short- and long-term memory.

- *Use multisensory materials whenever possible.* Primary grade teachers routinely use manipulatives with young children, who are concrete and literal minded in their thinking. Teachers of older children may not feel this is necessary and, as content becomes more abstract, may have more difficulty in finding such materials. As a consequence, many slip into a predominantly lecture or discussion mode of teaching. It is good to remember that, as adults, most of us prefer it and learn better when lecture or discussion is supplemented by hands-on involvement. Most of us capped our postsecondary classroom learning experiences with practica or internships to consolidate our abstract learning with the daily demands of our chosen professions.

- *Use applied situational learning whenever possible.* Roleplaying, simulations, unit teaching, or creative writing projects are preferable to isolated subject-oriented drill and practice because of the interest and personal meaning they provide. Time limitations and curriculum requirements may prevent teachers from making a total commitment to this teaching style, but all should strive for some balance between the two teaching approaches.

- *Use visualization to enhance meaning. Telling children to "Close your eyes and picture _____" and saying, "Can you see _____?" as well as, "Can you tell me about _____?"* will increase the likelihood that a visually oriented child can retain and retrieve information through the imaging process. Since a high percentage of the crossover children appear to use visuo-spatial processing of auditory input (i.e., they try to picture it), visualization is particularly adapted to this specific trait.

- *Use group response techniques to maintain involvement.* Rather than calling only on individuals during discussion, intersperse such directions as,"Everyone who agrees raise your right hand," or "Let's all point to the place in the book that tells us how Jean solved the mystery."

INCREASING SOCIAL SKILLS

The development of social skills is one of the most critical areas of need for children with learning disabilities, crossover children, and, in some instances, gifted children. Looking back on my experiences with college students with learning disabilities at Wright State University, a vivid memory is the overriding impression that they needed to develop social skills as well as academic ability to be successful in college and in later adult endeavors. For some of those students, the emotional baggage of having a learning disability proved overwhelming in the college setting. Others simply did not know how to approach professors and support personnel to get needed assistance without alienating the source of that assistance. Still others were unable to form friendships and become part of the college social scene. Those who did come to the university with a good sense of self, appropriate social skills, and an ability to function independently in a strange environment most often succeeded in spite of the challenge of coping with significant academic problems.

Many teachers and parents who are faced with a child with social problems have expressed their frustrations with these deficits. Most of us learned politeness, exchanging pleasantries, adjusting between everyday and Sunday-best behavior, and using common sense to cope with daily life incidentally (with a little help from our parents.). Most teachers expect "civilized" behavior from children and do not plan to spend much time teaching behavior that should have been learned at home. One type of learning disability, probably associated with frontal lobe dysfunction, impairs the learning of just such behavior in spite of the efforts of significant adults. Lerner (1985) described the characteristics of social disability as lack of judgment, difficulties in perceiving how others feel, problems with making friends, problems with establishing family relationships, difficulties in relating to teachers, and having a poor self-concept.

Social Skills Training

It is difficult to understand that a child may not be able to differentiate between a smile and a frown or between seriousness and playfulness, but such deficiencies do occur. Social skills can be taught in much the same way as academic skills. A structured plan is required. The content may be chosen from those skills most needed by the child, or, if a commercially available program is used, a group of children can be taken through a predetermined curriculum. Gesten, Weissberg, Amish, and Smith (1987) reviewed programs developed to assist children with social disabilities. Some programs relied heavily upon the behavioral and cognitive behavioral strategies discussed earlier in this chapter. Additionally, teacher-led discussions, homework activities, puppets, role-playing, using videotaped models, and videotaping children so that they may see their own behaviors were mentioned as common approaches.

DEVELOPING A POSITIVE SELF-CONCEPT

Self-concept refers to one's perception of oneself. It may be positive or negative, fantasy- or reality-based. The goal should be that each individual realistically appraise personal strengths and weaknesses and come to appreciate that, warts and all, he or she is a worthwhile human being. Being different from others can complicate the attainment of this goal. Therefore, self-appreciation and self-esteem may need to be taught. Commercial programs such as *Developing an Understanding of Self and Others (DUSO-2)* (Dinkmeyer,1982) and *Toward Affective Development (TAD)* (Dupont, Gardner, & Brody, 1974) are available for classroom or small group use. Teachers may use them alone or enlist the assistance of school counselors or psychologists. Other ideas can easily be incorporated into classrooms when teachers perceive the need to do so. Listed here are a few examples of activities that can fit easily into classroom or individual instructional settings. See Canfield (1976) or Frey and Carlock (1989) for many more examples.

- *Personal mailboxes.* Designate a place in the school where everyone—including the principal, secretary, cooks, and custodian—has a mailbox that can be used to deposit notes of praise. Something as simple as "Thanks for cooking pizza every Tuesday" or "Good for you! You stayed in line while going to the restroom today!" can be a gentle reminder to both adults and children that it is easy and rewarding to catch each other being good. Of course, in the case of children with multiple behavior problems, adults may have to ensure that the mail keeps coming.

- *Verbal praise.* Hopefully, anonymous written praise will generalize to a verbal support system. When the adults at school or at home set the focus on positive behavior in children and treat them with respect, this approach generalizes to other children. It is easy to get the "feel" of a school; it seems to permeate every part of the building. Usually, this feel is a direct result of the orientation of the principal and staff toward the children. Mutual respect multiplies and flowers and is joyful to observe!

- *Strength bombardment.* This technique can provide a needed extra dose of esteem building. The target child can sit in the middle of a circle of peers while they share what each one likes about the child in question. Teachers can model the broad range of possibilities by admiring an item of clothing or the way the child said "Thank you," after allowing him or her to borrow a pencil. The teacher or a scribe can write down the bombardment items, which can be kept on the child's desk, folded away in a bookbag, or displayed on a school or home bulletin board. Checking the list on a "down" day is a good way to bring things back into balance.

- *Letter to myself.* Frey and Carlock (1989) described this technique in which the child or adult writes him or herself a letter praising the self-growth made, continuing concerns ("I am concerned about . . .") and future goals ("I want to . . ." or "I am making progress on . . ."). The letter is collected by the teacher or counselor and mailed to the writer some time later. This serves as a good indicator of progress on the stated goals and concerns and the self-praise can brighten the sender/receiver's day. Self-appreciation is a great gift to give to oneself.

- *Bibliotherapy.* It is helpful to realize that we are not alone in the problems that we face. This need may be magnified by either giftedness or learning disability. The reading of biographies or fictionalized accounts of people facing problems similar to our own can provide encouragement, suggestions on how to cope, and the recognition that we are not alone. The literature of both special and gifted education points with pride to those who began with problems similar to those of the crossover child but later rose to fame because of their adult accomplishments. Not only do these accounts admonish us to never lose hope for our most troubled charges, they can also provide students with guidance and hope for their own futures. Reading to or having a child read about the short and painful school career of Edison or the lonely childhood of Eleanor Roosevelt can lead to self-understanding. Discussing a child's understanding of these famous lives may help to clarify personal issues, but an adult must curb a natural tendency to moralize or point out the similarities between subject and reader. Those conclusions are better reached and applied on the child's own terms. Local libraries have references that list books for children and adolescents under specific problem headings and age groups. One four-volume series that provides a guide to age-appropriate books for various problems is *The Bookfinder* (Dreyer, 1977–1989).

- *Visual imagery.* Our clinical findings suggest that visual imagery is a particular strength of the typical crossover child. In behavioral as well as academic matters, imagery can be used to set goals, reduce anxiety and stress, and provide an escape from unpleasant surroundings and circumstances. Many children must endure long bus rides to school or need to put behind them the memories of stressful mornings at home. Starting each day with a short imagery activity will prepare the class to become better learners and to start the workday in a better and more focused state of mind. Children should be instructed to close their eyes if they are comfortable doing so, sit in a comfortable position, and listen to the description provided by the teacher. Scripts of pleasant images are available in many places (e.g., Bagley & Hess, 1984; Eberle, 1971, 1982). Once the skill of imaging has been established, children can establish their own favorite places. A command to "go to your secret place" might help an anxious student to retreat momentarily from the stresses of reality, returning as a more productive learner. Just as a movement corner was suggested for hyperactivity, an imaging or imagining spot (such as a beanbag chair or other comforting enclosure) could be used to great advantage by many children.

CONTROLLING SOCIALLY INAPPROPRIATE BEHAVIORS

Verbal Bullying

Many of the problems discussed so far emanate from the disability rather than the giftedness of the crossover child. One characteristic that is more commonly observed in the gifted group is the tendency to flaunt their ability and verbally "bully" their peers of more average ability. Crossover children may not recognize their giftedness, but they may use some form of bullying or "put down" as a defense against personal feelings of inadequacy. Since the common response of other children is to isolate, ignore, or ostracize the bullying child, it is a behavior that needs to be extinguished.

Many gifted children who exhibit this behavior may be reflecting a sense of intellectual superiority instilled in them by their parents. These children may be victims of being reinforced only for their brainpower at the expense of their humanity. When parents focus all of their energy on the intellect of the child, they are developing a very narrow person. Frequently, the freewheeling fun of childhood is exchanged for a highly structured daily schedule that develops the child into an information bank with deficient social skills. Sometimes referred to as "hothousing," especially when it begins at an early age, this type of parenting presents a great danger to good mental health faced by many gifted children. Since hothousing is the product of well-meaning parents, professionals who observe information over-load in a child should be forceful in pointing out the potential problems. They must do so even though they are likely to become targets of parental denial and wrath. The professional might urge that, if gifted children are to become leaders, they need to develop their social skills as well as their intellect. This may be the rationale that best helps overzealous parents widen their vision of giftedness and their version of the role they should play in the child's development.

Bullies can be taught acceptable alternative responses and behaviors through some of the same modeling/coaching sequences described earlier. Teachers whose class-rooms function on a philosophy of mutual respect and where self-esteem-building activities are incorporated into the curriculum should encounter this behavior less frequently. Further, they may be able to extinguish it faster when it does appear than those who stress competition and individual achievement over cooperation and group success.

Perfectionism

This trait occurs at all ability levels, but it appears to be a plague among bright children. It is a trait that concerns parents of gifted children and appears to occur often in the crossover population. Given their academic deficiencies, perfectionism may present a greater problem for the latter group than for gifted children who do not have disabilities. The poor spelling and writing skills of crossover children result in messy, inaccurate papers. Most children with these problems are very aware of the differences between their written products and those of their classmates. The perfectionist wants a perfect product, a nearly impossible goal for the crossover child.

When perfectionism permeates every part of the child's life, careful monitoring and assistance may be necessary. Perfection is a goal no one can attain, so the perfectionist never lives up to her expectations. The female pronoun is used here since, unlike most other characteristics so far discussed, this trait seems to be more prevalent in girls than in boys. Although most parents insist that they do not impose perfectionism upon their children, emphasis on being a "good little girl" continues to exist in our society. Excessive "goodness" and a possession of high standards appear frequently at an early age. We know that eating disorders such as anorexia and bulimia often result from trying to be too good. Depression and even suicide may be contemplated by the child or adolescent who cannot live up to his or her own or others' standards. Since serious illness or death may result from these conditions, recognizing and treating perfectionism before, or early in, adolescence is important.

Adderholdt-Elliott (1987), in her book on this topic, suggests the following guidelines for recognizing and breaking the cycle of perfectionism. First, we need to differentiate between pursuing *excellence* (described as working hard, doing one's best, and feeling good about it) and *perfectionism* (described as working hard, doing one's best, and focusing in on minor mistakes or the work of the person who did slightly better). Second, we need to recognize that the ideal body, life, marriage, or career described in the media are ideals, not reality. Third, parents need to stop reinforcing a straight-A, win-or-nothing mentality so that children do not learn that receiving love is conditional upon getting all A's or winning an academic, music, or athletic contest. Fourth, we need to realize that procrastination and other paralyzed performance behaviors (such as writer's block) are signals of a perfectionist who, by not performing at all, cannot be open to criticism of the final product. Fifth, we need to realize that many physical and emotional symptoms accompany perfectionism. These warning signs of stress may include headaches, stomachaches, respiratory illnesses, sleep disorders, addictions, eating disorders, depression, and attempted suicide. These same symptoms are, of course, present when people are faced with other life stressors, but adults should be especially alert when they occur in a "good kid" who has "everything going for her."

To break the cycle of perfectionism, Adderholdt-Elliott (1987) suggests such steps as learning to fail (giving oneself permission to *not* succeed as a normal, necessary, and often desirable state), learning to laugh through the conscious pursuit of humor, taking risks by trying new activities in which one cannot excel, finding new friends who aren't perfectionists, prioritizing and accepting that neither "superkids" nor "superwomen" are possible or desirable, setting aside time for personal pleasure, and learning to reward oneself for practicing these new behaviors. In other words, she advocates working toward a well-rounded personality rather than accepting an overused brain, a neglected body, and an unhappy spirit.

"I Want to Be Like Everyone Else"

Whether it is articulated in words or evident in deeds, one goal of every exceptional child is to be liked and accepted by his peers. In our society, being average may be more highly encouraged and prized than being exceptional, although examples to the contrary do exist. Parents of any exceptional child can be expected to say, "I just want him or her to be normal." Because of the very conditions that have been identified as exceptional, the child is, in some sense, not "normal" and will never be so. The goal should not be normalcy (an elusive concept at best), but the development of a child and a family who both accept and value uniqueness and work hard to diminish the negative effects that may accompany that uniqueness. Denying exceptionality does not make it go away. Promising a child that we can "fix it and make it all better" is doing the child a great disservice. Treating giftedness as a disability diminishes the child's ability to use his or her gifts in a positive, productive way. Treating learning disability as a hindrance to a productive life increases the chances that the child will become an inadequate adult.

SUMMARY

Each of us has been dealt a certain hand to play in life. For those of us who, by chance or by choice, must deal with an exceptional child, our greatest gift to that child can be our encouragement to become the very best he or she can become without the added burdens of overconcern or unrealistic expectations. Careful attention to the social and emotional growth of each child should equal or exceed the importance we attach to academic progress.

References

Adderholdt-Elliott, M. (1987). *Perfectionism: What's bad about being too good.* Minneapolis: Free Spirit.

American Psychiatric Association. (1994). *Diagnostic and statistical manual of mental disorders* (4th ed.). Washington, DC: Author.

Ausubel, D. (1968). *Educational psychology: A cognitive view.* New York: Holt, Reinhart, & Winston.

Baddeley, A. (1986). *Working memory.* Oxford, England: Clarendon.

Bagley, M., & Hess, K. (1984). *200 ways of using imagery in the classroom.* New York: Trillium.

Camp, B., & Bash, M.A. (1985). *Think aloud: Increasing social and cognitive skills — A problem-solving program for children.* Champaign, IL: Research Press.

Canfield, J. (1976). *100 ways to enhance self-esteem in the classroom.* Englewood Cliffs, NJ: Prentice-Hall.

Cohen, G., Eysenck, M., & LeVoi, M. (1986). *Memory: A cognitive approach.* Philadelphia: Open University Press.

Das, J., & Varnhagen, C. (1986). Neuropsychological functioning and cognitive processing. In J. Obrzut & G. Hynd (Eds.), *Child neuropsychology, Vol. 1. Theory and research* (pp. 117–140). Orlando, FL: Academic Press.

Dinkmeyer, D. (1982). *Developing an understanding of self and others-2 (Rev.) (DUSO-2).* Circle Pines, MN: American Guidance Service.

Dreyer, S. (1977–1989). *The bookfinder* (Vols. 1-4). Circle Pines, MN: American Guidance Service.

Dupont, H., Gardner, O., & Brody, D. (1974). *Toward affective development.* Circle Pines, MN: American Guidance Service.

Eberle, B. (1971). *SCAMPER: Games for imagination development.* Buffalo, NY: D.O.K.

Eberle, B. (1982). *Visual thinking.* Buffalo, NY: D.O.K.

Frey, D., & Carlock, J. (1989). *Enhancing self esteem (2nd ed.).* Muncie, IN: Accelerated Development.

Gesten, E., Weissberg, R., Amish, P., & Smith, J. (1987). Social problem-solving training: A skills-based approach to prevention and treatment. In C. Maher & J. Zins (Eds.), *Psychoeducational interventions in the schools* (pp. 26–45). New York: Pergamon.

Hallowell, E., & Ratey, J. (1994). *Driven to distraction.* New York: Pantheon.

Kendall, P. (1988). *Stop and think workbook.* Merion Station, PA: Philip Kendall.

Lerner, J. (1985). *Learning disabilities: Theories, diagnosis, and teaching strategies (4th ed.).* Boston: Houghton Mifflin.

MacInnes, W., & Robbins, D. (1987). Brief neuropsychological assessment of memory. In L. Hartlage, M. Asken, and J. Hornsby (Eds.), *Essentials of neuropsychological assessment* (pp. 175–196). New York: Springer.

Meichenbaum, D. (1977). *Cognitive-behavior modification: An integrative approach.* New York: Plenum.

Silver, L. (1992). *The misunderstood child: A guide for parents of children with learning disabilities* (2nd ed.). Blue Ridge Summit, PA: TAB Books.

Simon, H. (1986). The role of attention in cognition. In S. Friedman, K. Klivington, & R. Peterson (Eds.), *The brain, cognition, and education* (pp. 105–115). Orlando, FL: Academic Press.

Squire, L. (1986). Memory and the brain. In S. Friedman, K. Klivington, & R. Peterson (Eds). *The brain, cognition, and education* (pp. 171–202). Orlando, FL: Academic Press.

Swanson, H. L., Cochran, K., & Ewers, C. (1990). Can learning disabilities be determined from working memory performance? *Journal of Learning Disabilities, 23,* 59–67.

Weiss, G., Hechtman, L. (1986). *Hyperactive children grown up.* New York: Guilford.

Webb, J., & Latimer, D. (1993, July). ADHD and children who are gifted. *ERIC Digest* (EDO-EC-93–5). Reston, VA: The Council for Exceptional Children.

4

Academic Intervention

He is a good student in science. I don't know how he knows so much when he can't read the textbook.

I call on her and she just looks at me. It's as though the words have to work their way through a brain fog before she can respond.

When I work with him one-on-one, I'm amazed at how well he can do. In the classroom, he seems overwhelmed and at a loss to know where to start.

One basic premise of this book is that the teaching of strategies for learning must accompany the teaching of content. The literature now contains many models for accomplishing this. The specific test patterns and learning styles that seem to prevail in crossover children indicate that holistic teaching methods are the approach of choice for these students. In some sourcebooks, holistic teaching might be termed *multisensory* or *integrated* and, in spite of the interest in "right-brained" and "whole-brained" learning in the last decade, most of the ideas are not new. The underlying premise of these ideas is that the traditional way in which teachers talk and students are encouraged to respond, either verbally or on worksheets, is not appropriate for children whose weaknesses lie in the integrational and attentional areas. The auditory/verbal, visual, and tactile/kinesthetic senses need to support each other and need to be employed in a meaningful context to overcome the most common weaknesses of the crossover child. When teaching these children, it is good to remember the words of Confucius:

> *I hear and I forget,*
>
> *I see and I remember,*
>
> *I do and I understand.*

That succinct, ancient adage describes the necessity and strength of the holistic, multisensory approach to teaching more eloquently than a lengthy academic discussion ever could.

Crossover children may be taught in regular, gifted, or special education classrooms or in one-to-one situations by tutors or parents. It is certainly possible to select specific techniques, some of which are described here, to address specific deficits.

First, a conceptual model is presented that compares the usefulness and appropriate application of clinical or prescriptive teaching to the cognitive strategies approach. A balance of both should be used to provide the knowledge base and the means to acquire new learning on one's own within and beyond the classroom.

THE RELATIONSHIP OF CLINICAL TEACHING AND COGNITIVE STRATEGIES TEACHING

Clinical or prescriptive teaching has been the special education methodology of choice for many years. In this method, a specific academic problem is pinpointed and various activities are designed to overcome it. This approach can be effective in overcoming specific skill deficits, but it has been criticized for its limitations, especially with secondary students. Reid (1988), in her review of the state of the art of teaching children with learning disabilities, indicated that, by upper junior high grades, these students tend to plateau at about the fifth-grade level in reading, writing, and arithmetic, and they drop out at a staggering rate. Crossover children should exceed a fifth-grade level of achievement. However, crossover children who are being educated primarily in LD classes that exclusively use the clinical teaching model may not be exposed to a number of strategies and ideas that could prepare them for higher levels of achievement and postsecondary education.

Within the last decade, so-called cognitive strategies have gained popularity. The strength of these techniques lies in the basic premise that the child, not the adult, should be the instrument of structure and regulation. Through carefully sequenced teaching procedures and specific instruction in problem-solving behaviors, the learner is given the tools to solve both academic and behavioral problems. When these are combined with methods that remediate content deficits, a powerful instructional model emerges.

Table 4–1 compares the clinical teaching and cognitive strategies models as described by Lerner (1985) and Reid (1988). It is easy to see the differences between the two approaches and the importance of each.

TABLE 4–1
Comparison of Clinical Teaching and Cognitive Strategies

Clinical Teaching	Cognitive Strategies
1. Emphasizes specific skills	1. Emphasizes holistic, contextual learning
2. Emphasizes knowledge	2. Emphasizes procedures as the key to knowledge
3. Works better with individuals	3. Works better in groups (all learn from modeling and examples from each other)
4. Academic achievement is the primary goal	4. Student self-direction is the primary goal

SELECTING SPECIFIC STRATEGIES

Chapter 3 presented a number of "learning to behave" ideas that addressed the nonacademic needs of many exceptional children. Similar sequences have been developed to provide "learning to learn or think" opportunities. A general cognitive strategy model is provided, followed by many ideas that either stress the application of this model to specific basic skills or provide methods for teaching the necessary basic skills content. Most of the latter emphasize the holistic approach, but some represent old favorites that have withstood the test of time. There is no such thing as a good or bad teaching strategy. The critical and difficult challenge is to make the match between learner needs and the teaching/learning technique. Not every idea will fit every child or every teaching circumstance, but these ideas may narrow the search. Parents or teachers who find an intriguing strategy among those listed here are encouraged to return to the primary source.

COGNITIVE STRATEGY SEQUENCES

Collier and Hoover (1987) reviewed the literature and found the following steps commonly described for strategy teaching:

1. *Identify and define the strategy; explain when and why to use it.* (This might be called association and giving meaning.)

2. *Use analogies, metaphors, common experiences or visual images to elaborate upon the verbal explanation.* (Provide multisensory input to ensure better storage.)

3. *Lead a group discussion about the uses of the strategy.* (Facilitate a participatory elaboration upon the first step.)

4. *Provide guided practice in using the strategy.* (Lay down memory tracks through repetition and practice.)

5. *Provide feedback while monitoring the use of the strategy.* (Ensure storage of accurate information.)

6. *Provide generalization activities.* (Associate with previously learned information and encourage the use of the strategy in new situations.)

Harris and Pressley (1991) believe that strategy instruction fulfills the constructivist theory that "real understanding occurs when children participate fully in the development of their own knowledge, and describe the learning process as self-regulated transformation of old knowledge to new knowledge" (p. 392). "First the adult provides support sufficient for the child to carry out the strategy, with guidance diminished as competence increases . . ." (p. 392), an approach that is sometimes referred to as *scaffolding.*

TEACHING BASIC SKILLS

Language Arts

The Whole Language Approach

One of the most promising advances in recent language arts teaching is known as the whole language approach. Part of its power comes from its origination with language arts specialists and its successful application to general as well as special education. When more educators become proficient in teaching this way, children who flounder in a curriculum that separates reading, writing, grammar, and spelling into disjointed, unrelated activities may survive in the regular classroom with little or no special education intervention.

In 1988, two excellent articles discussed the application of whole language to the needs of individuals with learning disabilities (Hollingsworth & Reutzel, 1988; Reutzel & Hollingsworth, 1988). The first article traces the history of whole language and compares it to the traditional subject-oriented approach. Whole language proponents view the language process as indivisible and advocate teaching beginning reading through various forms of literature or from environmental objects such as cereal boxes. It is their contention that this parallels the way we learn our spoken language. Immersion in a language-rich environment will shape a child's first inaccurate attempts at reading and writing into acceptable forms, just as "Me want!" gradually becomes "I want some more milk, please."

Part of the attractiveness of this approach for crossover children is that the "whole language classroom" described by Reutzel and Hollingsworth (1988) could just as well be a description of a typical gifted resource room. They describe an informal and comfortable place where desks are shoved aside in favor of beanbag chairs and rocking chairs. Activities center around a theme rather than a textbook, and all children are contributing to the in-depth study of that theme. If children are grouped, it is because of common interests, not tested reading level. A noisy, busy atmosphere replaces one of "stay in your own seat and do your own work."

In whole language classrooms, teachers model writing by sharing their compositions along with those of the class. They praise *trying* over *correctness*, urging that continued trying will eventually produce a "correct" product. They read literature and poetry to the children. Parts of their favorites are put on charts for group reading. Study of phonics and instruction in other reading skills result from the needs identified during the group reading. Much time is spent in Sustained Silent Reading (SSR) (periods of quiet time in the classroom when everyone is reading chosen material). Self-determined topics and cooperative work on language tasks are encouraged.

Hollingsworth and Reutzel (1988) suggested that the whole language approach may be more appropriate for children with learning disabilities than the traditional focus on the sequential introduction of predetermined specific skills. Consistent with the clinical findings discussed in this book, they hypothesize that the isolation of specific skills out of context may, contrary to its intent, magnify the learning problems of many children. Part of the difficulty may lie in the child's inability to make sense out of an artificial system. On the other hand, the whole language approach provides a systematic way of developing language arts skills by using the child's strengths, abilities, and interests.

The Writing Process

An integral part of the whole language approach is the writing process. In this process, the developmental cycle of good writing is acknowledged, taught, and encouraged. The steps involved are prewriting, or the first draft (getting thoughts down without interruption or attention to mechanics); a teacher/student conference when suggestions are made for revision including all of the traditional spelling, grammar, and neatness concerns; and a second draft, which is submitted to a peer or teacher for review and publication. The latter may take the form of a complete book or a simple essay that can be posted in the classroom (Graves, 1983). Graves

(1989a, 1989b, 1990, 1991, 1992) has written a series of handbooks for teachers that elaborate upon ways to use various types of writing to develop a "literate classroom."

Many crossover children have difficulty organizing their thoughts into sequences or cannot elaborate upon basic ideas. Providing a structure for planning stories can be helpful. Webbing (described later) or using story grids may be helpful. Crealock (1993) outlined a nine-stage process, from selecting story elements to completing the final draft. The first step she suggested was to provide lists of possible story elements under the topics Plot/Action (e.g., swim, fly), Hero (Superman, Fred), Heroine (Wonder Woman, Mom), Feeling (bored, shocked), Place/Location (Florida, moon), Thing (ghost, ring), and Time (noon, April). The lists under each element can be developed by the teachers and the students. The students can then randomly select elements and begin to flesh out their stories. Leavell and Ioannides (1993) used a similar support system to teach character development by focusing on the physical appearance, speech, actions, thoughts, and emotions of each character as he or she approached a problem-solving situation.

Literature-Based Reading

An integral part of the whole language approach is reliance on literature rather than textbooks. Mandlebaum, Lightbourne, and VanderBroek (1994) discuss the advantages of such an approach, whose characteristics accommodate the crossover child extremely well. They suggest that trade books, magazines, and newspapers are more effective teaching tools for several reasons. They provide more current information than textbooks. They are more flexible in matching the interests and ability level of the reader. They provide varied viewpoints and a greater depth of information. They increase student motivation because students may help select the materials. Further, they suggest that the language in literature is more natural since it is not under the constraints of a controlled reader. They argue that real reading and writing activities can be developed rather than using workbooks.

Mindmapping, Webbing, or Clustering

Some children and adults may find it helpful to develop outlines when they are planning a term paper or creative writing project. Others may find it easier to create a mind map, web, or cluster. While slightly different, each of these techniques consists of developing a loosely structured "picture" of one's emerging thoughts that will enhance the flow of one's ideas. The most detailed of the three processes is Buzan's (1976) *mind mapping*. He encourages the use of colored pens (as many as eight) to develop the map. The content of the map begins with a picture of the main topic in the center of the page in multicolor. Surrounding this multicolored drawing (used to engage the visuo-spatial and color centers of the brain) can be additional word/drawing combinations that indicate different random, but related thoughts generated by the writer or, if in a lecture situation, specific points made by the speaker. In recalling material mapped from the words of others, the "picture" of the page as well as the words come to mind, so that more complete recall is possible. Some persons who use this technique divide the page vertically, with the left two-thirds for the mind map and the right one-third for traditional or random notes that do not easily fit into the map.

Clustering or webbing involves the same concepts as mindmapping, but it is usually confined to single-color, words-only clusters. For example, a teacher of second and third grade gifted students was observed introducing a unit on American Indians by clustering the topics the class most wanted to investigate. Through this semi-

FIGURE 4–1
Web Generated by Second and Third Grade
Gifted Students in Mechanicsburg, Ohio

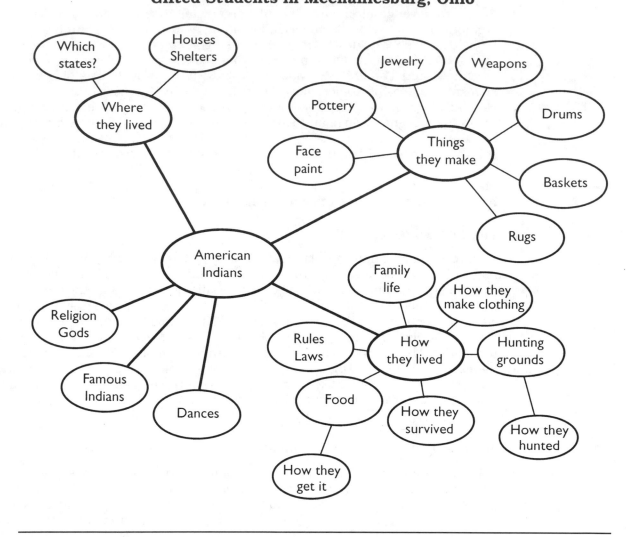

Source: Reprinted by permission of Patricia Archer.

controlled brainstorming procedure, these webbing novices were able to fill two panels of a chalkboard with their ideas. Their first attempt at webbing is reproduced in Figure 4–1 with the permission of their teacher. This same classroom was visited 3 weeks later. Working with a permanent copy of the web as their guide, the children had completed a map of the United States that contained the location of the Indian tribes, built replicas of the houses of specific tribes, and completed cloth costumes decorated with color from natural dyes. The holistic nature of this thematic study was evident even to an infrequent visitor.

If this process is used for creative writing, overlapping parts of the web can be grouped, organized, and sequenced so that a flow of ideas can come directly from the web or cluster. Two excellent resources for learning this approach are Rico (1983) and Pehrsson and Robinson (1985). Many other types of "graphic organizers" exist. Some will be explained in the discussion of content subjects.

Journal Keeping

Personal diaries can be used in the classroom for writing practice. The rules of confidentiality must apply, and children should understand that the content will remain known to the child and teacher only. The theory behind classroom journal keeping is similar to that of sustained silent reading (SSR)—that is, a child becomes a better writer by practicing writing on a daily basis. Use of this technique must be tempered by common sense when a motor deficit causes a child to develop a true aversion to writing.

Journal keeping is an application of the concept that the best learning comes from content with personal meaning. Children have the option of putting their most private and precious ideas on paper. Teachers can find clues to the emotional needs of their students through this process. Each day the teacher should respond to the child's thoughts in writing. When major issues arise (children may divulge in writing those experiences which are too painful to speak aloud), the teacher can, in writing, invite the child to talk about them. However, the control must remain in the hands of the child if the journal is to be a tool of empowerment. It is also true that teachers can make notes from which followup lessons on spelling, grammar, and punctuation can evolve; but the journal itself should not be marked or graded. Journal keeping allows the teacher to provide instruction in a gentle, personal way. Regard the difference in saying,"I have noticed in a number of your journals that you are having trouble knowing when to use a capital letter. Page 27 of this grammar book gives us some guidelines for solving this problem. Let's look at what it says and practice the sentences at the bottom of the page. Then, for the next three days, I want you to pay particular attention to capitalization when we do our journal writing," as opposed to, "Let's open our grammar books to page 27 and see what we're going to practice today." An excellent guide to using journals for a variety of purposes is *Journal Keeping with Young People* by Steiner and Phillips (1991).

Writing Metaphorically

Another technique that improves social-emotional behavior as well as language skills is that of writing metaphors. Metaphors provide a link between the known and the unknown. Frey (1986) encouraged the use of metaphors with gifted children because they enjoy abstract thinking and they resist being told directly the solution to a problem. Given the visualization, abstraction, creativity, and indirectness of the metaphor, it may indeed be the perfect technique for teaching crossover children. If jumping right into metaphorical writing seems difficult for children, start with a study of *Aesop's Fables*, which are, of course, marvelous metaphorical stories.

A Listening Skills Sequence

Forster and Doyle (1989) outlined this strategy sequence for increasing the listening skills of ADHD students. They report that it was highly effective in increasing quiz scores, notetaking skills, and increased awareness of current events when used with 30 adolescents with learning disabilities.

1. Tape a weather forecast, news item, and sports item from the morning news.

2. Prepare an outline of the content and a quiz on the material. (The Reds _____ the game last night. The score was _____.) Include higher-level questions as well as factual knowledge. (I believe the local environment would be less polluted if _____.)

3. Establish the purpose for the class. (E.g., Listen for main ideas, increase listening skills, and/or increase awareness of local and world events.)

4. Give the students the outline and tell them to circle any words they cannot read or do not understand. Explain these words.

5. Have the students listen to the tape and underline the key facts.

6. Clarify any unclear concepts.

7. Put away the outlines and have the students reconstruct the outline while the teacher writes it on the board. Compare the two versions.

8. Have the group summarize the outline, and have a scribe or the teacher write down the summary.

9. Give the quiz, grade it, and note any gaps in learning for future teaching.

TREE

Graham and Harris (1989) used the mnemonic TREE for encouraging the writing of better essays. The use of this prompt was embedded in an instructional sequence much like the one described at the beginning of this chapter. TREE stands for *Topic* sentence, *Reasons*, *Examining* reasons (will my readers buy my argument?), and *Ending*.

Use Language Arts "Quickies"

These are short exercises gleaned from a variety of places that seem to address one or more of the needs of the crossover child.

- *Study and illustrate sayings.* Examples include, "She coughed her head off," or "He had a frog in his throat" (Grady, 1984, p. 70). Think of the humor that children who often find learning such a serious business can express with this activity!

- *Write riddles instead of the usual dictionary definitions to describe new vocabulary words* (Grady, 1984, p. 71).

- *Use erased texts to highlight a certain part of speech.* Duplicate passages from a reading text, then erase all of the nouns, verbs, and so on. This is a variation of the Cloze procedure in which every seventh or ninth word is eliminated to check comprehension (Giordano, 1985).

- *Use comic strips as motivators.* Begin with comics such as *Henry* or *Nancy* which use little language and have obvious visuals. Progress to more detailed favorites such as *Peanuts* or *Garfield* by pasting blank balloons over the author's dialogue. Children with artistic gifts may wish to progress to their own creations. Many creative artists were not unlike our crossover children in their own childhoods. Mike Peters, Pulitzer prize winning cartoonist for the *Dayton Daily News* and creator of *Mother Goose and Grimm,* has shared his difficult school days with some of our local gifted children. Part of the inspiration for completing this book came from hearing his confession that his high school teachers admonished him frequently by saying, "Quit drawing those cartoons and do your work. You'll never be able to make a living drawing cartoons."

- *Study the Dolch words.* While this idea violates the holistic theme, persons not trained in remedial education do not always know the importance of the Dolch words. These are the 220 words most frequently used in grades 1 through 3 as identified by Dolch (1953). Not only are they the most common, but many are phonetic and spelling irregulars, so that they are particularly difficult for most children with learning disabilities. Anyone working with a child with language arts difficulties should assess that child's knowledge of the Dolch list and systematically work with the unknown words in as many creative, contextual ways as possible. While individual word cards may or may not be useful, having the child circle all of the "their"s in a given passage or advising the child that you will be marking all of the misspellings of "don't" and "does" in a given week will help highlight and correct misreading and misspellings to a manageable few at a time.

- *Use the neurological impress method.* This technique is helpful in breaking word by word reading habits in children who have struggled through oral reading for a prolonged period of time. The teacher and child should read a book simultaneously while the teacher's finger moves directly below the words being read in a slow, continuous motion. The teacher's voice and finger "pull" the child and encourage fluid reading. It is helpful to use a book that is interesting to the child and within the upper level of the child's reading ability. The process should be continued for a maximum of 15 minutes daily. No comprehension quizzing should follow (Heckelman, 1986).

- *Practice critical listening.* Alert children that you will be saying some things incorrectly (the errors may be grammatical or factual). Encourage them to raise their hands when an error occurs (Lerner, 1985, p. 336). Incidentally, this is also a "focus in" technique that should assist the distractible child.

- *Read television scripts.* Some television programs will release copies of their scripts for use in classrooms or, in this day of VCRs, volunteers may be able to type short excerpts of scripts directly from the tapes. Scripts are highly motivational in content and should help with fluency and expression. The process can be varied occasionally to include viewing the tape before or after reading the script.

- *Do choral reading.* Just as with neurological impress, the use of choral reading can break word-by-word reading habits and will assist in the development of better expression.

- *Restructure the reading circle.* Individual oral reading, except for diagnostic purposes, may not be defensible beyond second or third grade. In assessing your own mature reading pattern, you will find that you frequently skip over or misread many minor words, but are still able to comprehend the reading. Comprehension, not perfect word-by-word pronunciation, should be the goal. Many well-meaning teachers reinforce the wrong habits in poor readers by prolonging oral reading.

Whenever a reading circle is used, these techniques can enhance comprehension and participation. First, have the teacher read the passage to the children while they follow along. Then have them read it at their own pace and have them lightly mark with pencils those words they do not know. Comprehension can be checked by having the children read specific phrases or sentences that answer specific questions (rather than a sing-song round robin). As a last step, discuss and practice the individual unknown words. Distractible children should benefit from the constant involvement required in this process. At their seats, the children can once again read the passage to reinforce the newly learned words. In this approach, reading is taught as a silent skill used for comprehension, rather than a word-calling exercise of limited meaning or usefulness.

Handwriting and Spelling

Two of the biggest language arts problems in crossover children seem to be handwriting and spelling. Several factors contribute to these weaknesses. Foremost is the place of writing in the hierarchy of language acquisition. Language begins with personal experience and progresses through listening, speaking, reading, and finally, writing (Lerner, 1985). The last in the sequence, writing is the most difficult skill. Just think for a moment of the process involved in spelling a word. Unlike reading, where the word is in front of us, we must retrieve it from memory. If the storage of the word is faulty because of reversal tendencies, sequencing problems, or inadequate or meaningless practice, the ability to bring up the right letters in the right sequence may be difficult. Children who do not have good visualization or good sequencing skills may have to rely on sounding out the word. Unfortunately, the irregularity of the English language makes this a partially successful endeavor at best. Given all of the possibilities for problems, spelling is the most difficult of the language arts for most children with learning disabilities, even those who may have been identified initially because of a reading problem. At issue, as well, may be the fact that a shift of emphasis from reading to writing remediation does not occur when the child's needs change.

Christenson, Thurlow, Ysseldyke, and McVicar (1989) studied 10 elementary schools and found that, on the average, children in special education spent about 20 minutes a day on composing and that the emphasis was on mechanics rather than content. Regular education students in the same study averaged 33 minutes of writing each day.

Once again, the whole language approach appears to be a viable curricular solution to this problem. One study that supports this contention was completed in Spain (Jimenez & Rumeau, 1989). Nearly 300 primary grade children were divided into three groups who were taught writing by the global-natural (holistic, meaning-oriented) method, the syllabic method, or the phonics method. Initially, all groups made many errors, although they were of different types. After nearly 2 years, the errors made by the global-natural group decreased significantly as compared to the other two groups. The researchers concluded that the infusion of meaning into the learning process is helpful for children in that children can appreciate the usefulness of writing as a communication tool. These results, of course, must be intepreted cautiously for English-speaking children because of the phonetic consistency of Spanish.

Handwriting is troublesome for many children with learning disabilities and, since it is a motor skill rather than an intellectual one, crossover children appear to have no advantage over their less able peers. Handwriting is the most important of those fine motor skills that begin with buttoning, tying, cutting, and coloring. Children who were delayed or had difficulty in these preliminary skills may be introduced to formal manuscript writing before being physically ready to hold a pencil, space letters, or copy from a book or chalkboard. If development continues to be out of step with instruction, writing skill may never catch up or, at best, it may be a slow, laborious task. Additionally, many children are either left handed and/or grip the pencil awkwardly and close to the lead. An awkward grip appears to slow down the writing process and fatigue the writer.

Other characteristics of learning disability exacerbate the writing problem. Impulsivity tends to cause quick, careless work. Unlike reading, which can be corrected immediately, the errors of careless writing leave a record of the weakness, sometimes in the form of frequent erasures. Children with visual-perceptual problems may find spacing and staying on or appropriately above or below the lines quite difficult. The near point/far point task of copying from the chalkboard may be unfair for those with eyes that do not adjust quickly to these two conditions or for those whose impulsivity or poor memory make copying letter by letter an ordeal. Finally, when one finds it difficult to express oneself or lacks the spelling skills to write thoughts on paper, production of the written word becomes a surefire way to be graded unfavorably. Few of us enter cheerfully into our personal areas of weakness!

Support for the prevalence and nature of writing disabilities in gifted children is found in the work of Yates, Berninger, and Abbott (1995). They distinguish between "*text generation,* or the translation of ideas into language representations in working memory" (pp. 132–133) and *transcription* or "translation of those representations into written symbols on the printed page" (p. 133). When comparing 10 gifted and 10 average students in each grade, 1 through 6, they found that the two groups did not differ in the number of words or clauses generated (low-level compositional fluency) or low-level syntactical complexity. The gifted students were significantly superior in vocabulary sophistication and composition quality (both of which were determined by a scoring rubric). When the students' performance on nine writing subskills was compared to the achievements expected for their IQ, 43.4% of the gifted students and 8.3% of the average students met the criterion for writing disability on at least one of the components. When compared on absolute criteria (low functioning independent of IQ), 11.7% of the gifted and 25% of the average children met the criterion. The researchers concluded that it is the inability to adequately represent their sophisticated thoughts on paper that causes frustration, avoidance, and lack of self-esteem in gifted children.

While the whole language approach may decrease the writing problems developed by children with learning disabilities, it is certain that, for some, the problem will continue to exist. It seems worthwhile to consider strategies that bypass handwriting rather than to spend long hours at remediation, particularly since remediation seldom has a positive result. Inherent in the following recommendations is the need for a concerted effort among special educators to convince administrators, other educators, and parents that these alternative strategies are necessary and appropriate for this subgroup of children.

To make a convincing argument for providing alternatives to handwriting, one can liken the prolonged teaching of this skill to a motor-impaired student to teaching reading to a child with vision impairment who is not wearing or cannot wear corrective lenses. Reluctant adults should be asked to list all of the ways in which they use the written word in their daily living. While it is a skill of considerable importance to students of any age, adult writing is mostly confined to shopping lists, checkbook entries, and the like. Most job or credit applications require typing or printing and, other than our signature, writing is an infrequent or optional adult activity. One must conclude that writing by hand is fast becoming an outmoded means of communication.

There are several compensatory approaches to handwriting that should be considered as early as second grade. While crossover children and those with more severe learning disability should participate in handwriting instruction in the early grades, they should be allowed to produce lengthy written assignments on typewriters or word processing computers as soon as they have the skills to do so. Keyboarding programs for primary students are now available and should be mandatory, especially for children with fine motor problems (see Appendix C). Delaying proper teaching until the intermediate grades or higher will mean that, for many, hunt-and-peck habits will have to be broken down and new skills learned. MacArthur (1988) contended that the use of word processing has social as well as academic implications for the student with learning disability in that a good, legible copy of material is more likely to be shared with peers or submitted for evaluation or publication.

The other advantage of computer writing is, of course, that word processors can be equipped with spelling and grammar correction programs. Remember, the only purpose for either handwriting or spelling is to convey ideas; they are not skills unto themselves. If spelling will be a lifelong deficiency, which commonly seems to be the case, then giving children the means to overcome this impedance to their creative and technical writing production seems sensible. Most working adults now must have some computer proficiency. Focusing on word processing rather than hand-writing will not deprive children with writing deficits; it will, in fact, bring them closer to the reality of their world.

Even if the recommendations presented here are implemented, the child, as student, will continue to be faced with considerable in-class writing. Giordano (1984) provided ideas for developing or remediating LD students' writing, including resto-ration (the Cloze procedure), outlining, and paraphrasing. For older students, mindmapping can be used for notetaking or lectures can be taped for later, slower notetaking, computer storage, or mindmapping. In extreme cases, a "buddy" notetaker who uses carbon paper can be recruited. Spelling can be facilitated by using personal lists or *The Quick-Word Handbook for Everyday Writers* (Sitton & Forest, 1994), an easily accessible list of 1,020 high-use writing words. When motor fatigue is a problem, permission should be given to write out answers only or to have a volunteer write down the questions and problems. Always, the point needs to be made for and with the child that these privileges are ways to help work around a *real* problem, not a reinforcement of lazy, "he could if he would" work habits.

Mathematics

Beginning mathematics may be a less frequent problem for children with learning disabilities than are the language arts. However, some crossover children will have problems with mathematics. Montague (1991) compared the mathematical prob-lem-solving strategies of three gifted middle school students and three crossover children. After instruction in think-aloud problem solving, the students were given specific problems and interviewed about the strategies used to solve them. Montague found that the crossover students were less confident about their ability, used fewer strategies, made more errors, and failed to paraphrase the problem (put it in their own words). She suggested that studying the strategies of gifted students and teaching them to crossover students may be a useful instructional approach.

Whenever possible, mathematics teaching should involve all of the senses. Most primary teachers use counting sticks, Cuisenaire rods, and tangrams in their teaching. Sometimes we need to look beyond these usual classroom trappings. In her workshop on holistic teaching, Barbara Meister Vitale has told the story of successfully teaching basic math facts to a group of streetwise kids in one afternoon once she began to use dice as the teaching tool.

When teaching or remediating mathematics for crossover children, the teacher needs to carefully assess the cause of any breakdown in achievement. Many children make errors in mathematics for the same reasons that they make errors in handwriting. Impulsivity, ignoring signs, spatial problems, and reversals tend to lead to faulty numerals and wavy columns, which in turn lead to inaccurate answers. Memory problems may impair acquisition of basic facts. Because each problem has to be counted out (often surreptitiously), completion of assignments becomes a major problem. A lack of practical application to reinforce book learning may impair the understanding of many children whether or not they have a learning disability. Certain approaches may minimize the effects of these factors. They include the following:

- Multisensory experiences for beginning mathematics concepts might include using classmates rather than sticks for counting, adding, and subtracting purposes. Ten children in the front of the classroom can be moved around in many marvelous, reinforcing ways. Large muscle activity may teach those concepts not being learned by pencil and paper exercises.

- The use of color to differentiate columns or distinguish between bundles of ones, tens, or hundreds can aid some children.

- Lindquist (1989), in *The National Council of Teachers of Mathematics 1989 Yearbook*, made several recommendations about changing the way in which mathematics is taught in this country. Two of her suggestions for aiding the child who has a memory disability or writing deficit are to increase emphasis on the variety of ways to compute and make estimates and to decrease the time used for paper and pencil computation. Until now, the conventional wisdom has been that children will not learn basic math facts if the calculator can do the work. Now, research is beginning to suggest that, as an error-free reinforcer, the calculator may actually speed up the learning process. Certainly, for the child with learning disabilities whose deficient retrieval of facts may slow down or even stop math progress, this device is an absolute necessity. Lindquist concluded, " It is time to educate youth in how to use the tools of today including their minds, paper and pencil, calculators, and computers" (1989, p. 6).

- One of the greatest needs in mathematics education seems to be raising awareness of applications in everyday life. To accomplish this, the teacher might ask crossover children to keep a 1-week list of every place they observe mathematics in action. From that list, a creative teacher could determine which skills are needed to perform the activities listed. It may also be helpful to determine which important skills are missing from the repertoires of the reporting children. Assuming that most had been introduced in previous teaching, a very focused remedial unit could be planned.

- The computer seems well-suited to the crossover child whose knowledge of basic mathematical skills and facts needs reinforcement. Paper and pencil drill and practice exercises may seem mundane, repetitious, and difficult because of the writing requirements, but they are needed by most crossover children. The graphics as well as the immediate feedback and reinforcement found in most computer programs increase their interest factor and make the necessary practice palatable. The availability of programs such as LOGO that stress problem solving, directionality, basic programming, and geometric concepts provides a challenge that can excite the intellect while reinforcing the needed skills.

- A critical point must be made about advanced mathematics and the college-bound high school student. My experience with college students with learning disabilities at Wright State University showed that a lack of a solid mathematical background is more likely to be a stumbling block in college success than is reading and writing, for which more compensatory strategies are available. The need for careful planning of educational goals at the eighth-grade level is of prime importance in mathematics because of the highly sequential nature of the discipline.

Content Subjects

In spite of basic skills deficiencies, most crossover children will like and will master content subjects. The interest factor and the holistic nature of the content tend to fit the strengths of these children. If the computer and other basic skills compensations are in place and the children are allowed to use them, true giftedness can blossom. We are just beginning to realize the benefits that access to information through CD-ROM material, computer link-ups to libraries, and other data sources will bring serious students. With the completion of a science fair project, an artistic display, or a computer-generated graphic, the creativity and intelligence of the crossover child is likely to emerge.

When studying textbooks is a necessity, two approaches can be used. For comprehension, SQ3R is an excellent way to control impulsivity, memory deficits, and lack of attention to detail. This is an old technique (Robinson, 1962) that predates the concept of strategies teaching, but it provides a set method for attacking content material. It can be used for students in the third grade and above. The steps suggested by the acronym include:

1. *Skim.* Before beginning the reading of a passage, look it over, see how long it is, check the charts or illustrations, and get a general idea of the topics covered.

2. *Question.* Look at the subheading that introduces the section you are about to read. Turn that heading into a question. (For example, "The products of Brazil," becomes "What are the products of Brazil?")

3. *Read.* Read the paragraphs under the subheading, looking for the answer to your question.

4. *Recite.* This can be described to children as "talking to oneself." Try to answer your question. If the answer comes very slowly or your response seems to be limited then try again.

5. *Review or reread.* Go back over the material until you are satisfied with your ability to answer the question.

Maring, Furman, and Blum-Anderson (1985) suggested a group cooperative learning strategy that fulfills much the same need as SQ3R. The group first writes down the headings or subheadings of a given assignment. Each person in the group brainstorms (predicts) what might be in the reading and a scribe writes this in a notebook. The group reads to confirm and/or revise its hypotheses. The notebook is revised or completed.

One of the main advantages of these two ideas is that they "chunk" assignments in much the same way that dashes in telephone and social security numbers help us to remember long numerical sequences. Most of us have had the experience of reading many pages of an assignment before realizing that we had not comprehended much, if any, of it. By refocusing on the content at the end of each section and by constantly using the heading question as a guide, this problem can be controlled. SQ3R can be a laborious process in the beginning for an individual learner. It is a good idea to assure students (and, if needed, their other teachers and parents) that it is better to read and comprehend 5 pages of a 10-page assignment than to read all 10 pages and comprehend nothing. In the beginning stages, this technique could be used for part of the assignment, then supplemented by a tape, a reader, or a peer tutor.

For reinforcement or organization of textbook or lecture material, a variety of *graphic organizers* can be used. One excellent series for elementary school children that combines science and social studies content with the teaching of graphic organizers and other process skills is *Breakthroughs: Strategies for Thinking* (Zaner-Bloser, 1990). This series teaches the selection of certain organizers for specific purposes or content. For instance, *interaction frames* might be used to graphically compare the goals of two different groups, the action/reaction of each group to the other, and the possible outcomes for each group. The events leading to the war in the Middle

East fit nicely into this schema. The teacher's manual for the series gives suggestions for interfacing a number of other organizers and thinking skills with the provided content. The attractive format and content of this series make it highly adaptable for regular classrooms and ideal for LD or gifted resource units.

In another example of using organizers, Cunningham and Cunningham (1987) described a teacher-prepared *study matrix* as a guided learning experience in a content area. A matrix compares the relationship of two sets of information. To study the planets, the names of the planets could be placed on the page vertically, and across the top such characteristics (as compared to Earth) as "closer to sun," "larger," "has moons," "has rings," and "time required to orbit sun" could be written. Students fill in those items which they know on the matrix, then read to correct and complete the matrix. As a last step, a summary of the characteristics of each planet is written.

A specific technique for studying history was described by Kinder and Bursick (1993). They used a strategy entitled *problem-solution-effect analysis* to link historical facts and concepts. For instance, the invention of the cotton gin facilitated removal of seeds from American cotton, increased production, and led to the need for more slaves to plant and harvest the crop, leading to another set of problems. Isolated factual information such as timelines and vocabulary were linked to the conceptual framework.

Learners who understand their own deficiencies and are given specific ways to compensate for them are more likely to be successful than those who are taught only to rely on the assistance of adults. Without such strategies, upon removal of that assistance, they may find themselves at a loss and may never reach their potential. It is a good example of teaching a man to fish rather than giving him a fish when he is hungry.

SUMMARY

The ideas presented in this chapter are but a sampling of those available, but they do represent a framework from which you can build your own strategies or look for those of others. No one approach will work for everyone, and a variety of ideas and repetitions is needed by everyone. The references for this chapter are good sources of additional ideas and resources.

Finally, in those instances when crossover children are successful, praise them and let them shine! Nothing diminishes a good try more than the pronouncement of some adult that "See! I knew you could do it if you would only try!" No one functions at peak efficiency consistently, but when a particularly good effort is put forth by a child with disabilities, share the child's joy and acknowledge to yourself the level at which he or she can function under proper motivation. Assuming that high self-esteem can be kept intact, adults tend to pick those vocations which reward them frequently; so look upon each success as a firm foundation for later adult success and happiness.

References

Buzan, T. (1976). *Use both sides of your brains.* New York: Dutton.

Christenson, S., Thurlow, M., Ysseldyke, J., & McVicar, R. (1989). Written language instruction for students with mild handicaps: Is there enough quantity to ensure quality? *Learning Disability Quarterly, 12,* 219–229.

Collier, C., & Hoover, J . (1987). *Cognitive learning strategies for minority handicapped students.* Lindale, TX: Hamilton.

Crealock, C. (1993). The grid model for teaching narrative writing skills. *Teaching Exceptional Children, 25*(3), 33–37.

Cunningham, P., & Cunningham, J .(1987). Content area reading-writing lessons. *Reading Teacher, 40,* 506–512.

Dolch, E. (1953). *The Dolch basic sight word list.* Champaign, IL: Garrard.

Forster, P., & Doyle, B.(1989). Teaching listening skills to students with attention deficit disorders. *Teaching Exceptional Children, 21,* 20–22.

Frey, D. (1986). Using metaphors with gifted children. *English Language Arts Bulletin, 27,* 21–22.

Giordano, G. (1984). *Teaching writing to learning disabled students.* Rockville, MD: Aspen.

Giordano, G. (1985). Learning to read erased text. *Academic Therapy, 20,* 317–322.

Grady, M. (1984). *Teaching and brain research: Guidelines for the classroom.* New York: Longman.

Graham, S., & Harris, K. (1989). Improving learning disabled students' skills at composing essays: Self-instructional strategy training. *Exceptional Children, 56,* 201–214.

Graves, D. (1983). *Writing: Teachers and children at work.* Exeter, NH: Heinemann.

Graves, D. (1989a). *Experiment with fiction.* Portsmouth, NH: Heinemann.

Graves, D. (1989b). *Investigate nonfiction.* Portsmouth, NH: Heinemann.

Graves, D. (1990). *Discover your own literacy.* Portsmouth, NH: Heinemann.

Graves, D. (1991). *Build a literate classroom.* Portsmouth, NH: Heinemann.

Graves, D. (1992). *Explore poetry.* Portsmouth, NH: Heinemann.

Harris, K., & Pressley, M. (1991). The nature of cognitive strategy instruction: Interactive strategy construction. *Exceptional Children, 57,* 393–403.

Heckelman, R. (1986). N.I.M. revisited. *Academic Therapy, 21,* 411–420.

Hollingsworth, P., & Reutzel, D. (1988). Whole language and LD children, *Academic Therapy, 23,* 477–488.

Jimenez, J., & Rumeau, M. (1989). Writing disorders and their relationship to reading-writing methods: A longitudinal study. *Journal of Learning Disabilities, 22,* 195–199.

Kinder, D., & Bursick, W. (1993). History strategy instruction: Problem-solution-effect analysis, timeline, and vocabulary instruction. *Exceptional Children, 59,* 324–335.

Leavell, A., & Ioannides, A. (1993). Using character development to improve story writing. *Teaching Exceptional Children, 25*(4), 41–45.

Lerner, J. (1985). *Learning disabilities: Theories, diagnosis, and teaching strategies* (4th ed.). Boston: Houghton Mifflin.

Lindquist, M. (1989). It's time to change. In P. Trafton & A. Shulte (Eds.), *New directions for elementary school mathematics (1989 yearbook)* (pp. 1–23). Reston, VA: National Council of Teachers of Mathematics.

MacArthur, C. (1988). The impact of computers on the writing process. *Exceptional Children, 54,* 536–542.

Mandlebaum, L., Lightbourne, L., & VanderBroek, J. (1994). Teaching with literature. *Intervention in School and Clinic, 29,* 134–150

Maring, G., Furman, G., & Blum-Anderson, J. (1985). Five cooperative learning strategies for mainstreamed youngsters in content area classrooms. *Reading Teacher, 39,* 310–317.

Montague, M. (1991). Gifted and learning-disabled gifted students' knowledge and use of mathematical problem-solving strategies. *Journal for the Education of the Gifted, 14,* 393–411.

Pehrsson, R., & Robinson, H. A. (1985). *The semantic organizer approach to writing and reading instruction.* Rockville, MD: Aspen.

Reid, D.K. (1988). *Teaching the learning disabled: A cognitive developmental approach.* Boston: Allyn & Bacon.

Reutzel, D. R., & Hollingsworth, P. (1988). Whole language and the practitioner. *Academic Therapy, 23,* 405–416.

Rico, G. (1983). *Writing the natural way.* Los Angeles: J.P. Tarcher.

Robinson, F. (1962). *Effective reading.* New York: Harper.

Sitton, R., & Forest, R. (1994). *The quick-word handbook for everyday writers.* North Billerica, MA: Curriculum Associates.

Steiner, B., & Phillips, K. (1991). *Journal keeping with young people.* Englewood, CO: Teacher Ideas Press.

Yates, C., Berninger, V., & Abbott, R. (1995). Specific writing disabilities in intellectually gifted children. *Journal for the Education of the Gifted, 18,* 131–155.

Zaner-Bloser. (1990) *Breakthroughs: Strategies for teaching thinking.* Columbus: Author.

5

Academic Enrichment

She has an IQ of 128. It has to be wrong. She can't spell a thing! But she sure can tell me more than I want to know about dinosaurs!

He just seems to be off in some dreamworld when he should be doing math. I thought he had attention deficit, but the psychologist says he's just fantasizing about some mythical Superteam he has concocted. I wish he would concoct some math papers! The only time he comes alive is during computer period.

He's so sensitive. If anyone says the least little thing to him, he sulks the rest of the day and I can't get him back to work.

Just as the problems associated with learning disability must be addressed directly in order for crossover children to succeed, these children must be provided with opportunities to develop their gifted traits. Their minds need to be challenged through higher-level thinking and the content of an enriched or differentiated curriculum. This strikes me as the educational fulfillment of the popular admonition that we should give our children both roots and wings. Avenues for accomplishing this include providing curricular adaptations and teaching skills that facilitate critical and creative thinking. The enrichment processes discussed in this chapter are well known and widely used in gifted programs. Many can be adapted for other settings, especially if a collaborative inclusion team includes a gifted education specialist. Introduction to the skills described is important, regardless of whether they are taught by an LD, regular class, or gifted teacher.

CURRICULUM FOR THE GIFTED

VanTassel-Baska (1989) described the known principles of curriculum for the gifted as including different kinds of instruction, a greater depth of learning, the need for homogeneous grouping for at least part of the day, and differentiated services for the entire K–12 program. It is her belief that special programming can best be conceptualized from a traditional content base—that is, those gifted in mathematics should have access to mathematical principles and applications in greater breadth and depth than for other students and than they have access to in other areas. This targeted differentiation fits the disparate abilities of the crossover child very well.

VanTassel-Baska (1989) suggested that movement toward this ideal curriculum can be accomplished by deleting or compressing basic curriculum, concentrating on higher-level thinking skills, concentrating on interrelationships among bodies of knowledge, introducing nontraditional school subjects, encouraging self-directed learning, and encouraging a commitment to learning by providing access to and information about technology and its uses.

If access to curriculum that approaches these ideals is limited, special programs may be available that allow the crossover child to interact with other children on a higher level than is possible in the regular classroom. Local universities or school systems may offer Saturday or summer enrichment courses. In many of these programs, *doing* rather than book learning is emphasized; therefore,the reading/writing weaknesses of the crossover child will not be a disadvantage. Many school systems participate in academic competitions in nearly every content area. *Odyssey of the Mind* is a national competition that stresses the creative process (contact the OM Association, P.O. Box 547, Glassboro, NJ 08028 for information), and *Future Problem Solving* is a program based on the Creative Problem Solving Process described below (FPS International, 315 W. Huron, Suite 140B, Ann Arbor, MI 48103). It is important to search out opportunities that are available locally so that each child can participate in programs that best suit his or her particular needs.

MAJOR COGNITIVE OPERATIONS

Intelligent children must be taught the tools of intelligent thought if they are to apply their gifts appropriately. Beyer (1987) identified three such major cognitive operations: (1) thinking strategies that include problem solving, decision making, and conceptualizing; (2) critical thinking skills; and (3) micro-thinking skills such as those identified in Bloom's *Taxonomy of Educational Objectives* (Bloom, 1956) as well as reasoning skills. These skills are important for crossover children because they will help counteract a tendency to work quickly and faultily without attention to detail or concern about the quality of the end product. When used in a classroom group, thinking activities provide opportunities for crossover children to use and display their considerable verbal talents.

Creative Thinking

Ideas generated by the creative mind are characterized by quantity, variety, and complexity. Gifted educators incorporate into their curricula many specific activities that supposedly enhance the ability to think creatively. The true creative geniuses of any age are more likely born than made, but each of us has the potential of either losing or harnessing our own measure of creative potential. Use of the word *harnessing* is deliberate because, in the case of crossover children, much of their creative energy can be lost or diluted through their impulsivity and disorganization. *Unharnessed* creativity does not usually lead to a new invention, a lifesaving technique, or a beautiful poem. Even the impulsive Mozart eventually had to write down his music for it to survive. Most of us will not be able to duplicate the creativity of that child prodigy, of whom his father said, "The only problem was that it was difficult to teach him much because he already seemed to know everything by instinct" (Kupferberg, 1986). Instead, insistence upon a product that reflects care and planning as well as freewheeling idea generation is an important part of the development or maintenance of creativity. For this reason, teaching a creative problem-solving process is more beneficial than teaching "creativity." Treffinger (1990) stated that the appropriate question is not "Am I creative?" but "In what ways am I creative?" Modeling this attitude and combining it with the sequential teaching of a creative problem-solving process should ensure the recognition of the creative attributes of the crossover child.

Creative Problem Solving

A major force in developing and disseminating the concepts of creative problem solving (CPS) was Alex F. Osborn (1963). Eberle (1982) described Osborn, the founder of the Creative Education Foundation, as "an innovative advertising executive with a high sense of purpose. Dr. Osborn was seriously concerned about the difficulty and urgency of more fully releasing creativity and problem-solving ability in the individual human being" (p. 6). In the Foreword of the third edition of *Applied Imagination*, Osborn (1963) described such diverse settings as General Electric, Air Force ROTC, and numerous colleges as institutions that had incorporated his suggestions into their training programs. The author's own training took place in a group about evenly divided among business persons, military officers, and educators. A great personal insight gained from that experience was that a person from another discipline frequently generated a better solution than could the person presenting the problem. We are indeed thwarted in solving our own problems by our tendency to narrow our sights and prejudge our options! These are the barriers that CPS is designed to overcome.

The problem described here as an example is an adult one, one that many readers may share. The steps of the Creative Problem Solving Institute (CPSI) model are adapted from Noller (1977).

1. *The MESS.* The mess is a vague, gnawing problem that we want to solve. People often close options prematurely by identifying narrow, specific problems that contribute to the mess, rather than the mess itself.

   Example: I want to help my student, John, improve his grades.

2. *Fact Finding.* During this step we should brainstorm freely, writing down every bit of information we can think of that pertains to the problem.

   Examples:

   • John gets Bs in math, but Ds in language arts.

   • All teachers complain that he does not turn in his homework.

   • Rewarding John gets better results than punishing him.

   • His parents report that he knows the work at home, but he has forgotten much of it by the next day.

3. *Problem Finding.* This step clarifies the MESS based upon the information generated in the previous brainstorm. CPSI suggests that the stem "In what way might I" (IWWMI) be used as the basis for hypothesizing. As in the previous step, responses should follow the brainstorming rules of suspending judgment and "the sky's the limit."

   Example: IWWMI help John improve his grades?

   • His mother might attend class with him.

   • I might punish him for bad grades.

   • The school might hire a tutor.

   Pick one of the above and repeat the process.

IWWMI help John if his mother attends class with him?

- She might do his work for him.
- She might see his viewpoint as a student and be better able to help him at home.
- She might provide insight for me so that I might better help him at school.

IWWMI help John if his mother provides a different insight on him as a student?

After completing several levels of IWWMI, look over the ideas, then pick the one that best describes your real concern. The theory of brainstorming is that the most creative ideas come when you are pushing yourself to the limit, so do not stop this process too soon. Often the clarifying question will come in the later levels of the exercise.

4. *Idea Finding.* Once the "real" problem is identified, couch it in IWWMI terms.

   Example: Let's assume that the final question was, "In what way might I help John get more of his homework in on time and in acceptable form?"

   Brainstorm this question thoroughly, looking at real, unreal, possible, impossible, and unpredictable options.

   Responses that come to mind include the following:

   - Have his parents do it for him.
   - Have his parents take him and his homework to school each day.
   - Get him a computer.
   - Mail the homework to and from home.
   - Hire a tutor.
   - Have his father help him.
   - Teach him study skills.
   - Work out a reward system.

5. *Solution Finding.* From the list above, which may contain as many as 30 or 40 alternatives, pick about 5 that seem the most sensible to you. *Please note that this is the first time that good sense, evaluation, or other signs of judgment are used. The beauty of the CPS process is that it uses a flight of fancy (creative thinking) to come up with a workable, practical solution to a real problem.* After the alternatives are selected, a grid is set up that provides a matrix between the alternatives and evaluative criteria that you must choose. Table 5–1 shows a sample grid for the sample problem. Once the options and the criteria are in place, apply a numerical system of judgment to each column. In this example, 5 is used for "terrific," 3 for "good," and 1 for "poor." When you are finished with the evaluation, the alternatives with the highest value should give you a good starting place. In our example, the top two options, teach study skills and develop a reward system, could be combined to give John some new strategies and provide an incentive for learning and applying them.

6. *Acceptance finding.* Plans that suit you may not be suitable for others. For our solution to work, John, his parents, and his other teachers will need to be involved. Actually, it would have been better to follow the CPS steps as a group, but this is not always possible. To complete the process, decide what the first step will be and get started!

TABLE 5–1
A Creative Problem-Solving Evaluation Matrix

Alternatives	Criteria					
	Cost	Time	John like?	Dad Like?	Tchrs?	Total
Let father help	5	3	1	1	3	13
Hire a tutor	1	3	3	1	3	11
Take to school	3	1	1	1	1	7
Teach study skills	3	3	3	3	5	17
Use reward system	3	3	5	3	3	17

Criteria: 5 = terrific; 3 = good; 1 = poor choice

This example has attacked a behavioral problem from an adult viewpoint. Another alternative might have been to teach John the process and have him devise his own solution to his homework problem. Eberle and Stanish (1985) adapted the process for Grades 3 through 9 in *CPS for Kids*. Children are challenged to address such problems as what to do when locked out of the house without a key or how to keep friends while maintaining personal principles (not violating them when friends urge you to steal a candy bar from a local store).

CPS has similar application in content areas. In what way might we compare the dangers faced by the Pilgrims' crossing with those faced by modern astronauts? In what way might we introduce Benjamin Franklin to the use of a computer? The national Future Problem Solving program is based on applying CPS to national and international issues such as pollution, overpopulation, and world hunger. As noted earlier, crossover children who have mastered CPS might find great satisfaction in participating in Future Problem Solving activities.

Those who are naturally creative often bristle at the structure and stilted format of CPS. However, with practice, the steps come very rapidly and decision making can be done easily without relying on pencil and paper steps. When confronted with a major problem, returning to the formal multistep procedure can help inspire the creative process. The most important components of CPS are the suspension of judgment through the early stages and the eventual return to what is real and manageable.

Decision-Making Skills

The development of concepts is a basic purpose of schooling. When memorization of facts parades as learning, recall and use of such information beyond in-school test taking is rare. For concepts to take on long-term usefulness, a deeper level of understanding is needed. Beyer (1987) cited the identification of examples (horses and cows as mammals), the identification and classification of common attributes (they have hair, are warm-blooded, and nurse their young), and the identification of nonexamples (frogs and snakes) as component parts of this process. Much of the curriculum of the early grades entails concept development. A discussion of two subskills of concept development, observation and classification, follows to illustrate the importance of this process of learning.

Observation

The basis for all knowledge is what we receive through our senses (the five basic ones and those beyond such as awareness of temperature, atmospheric pressure, pain, etc.). Those of us with stick figure drawing skills wonder at the artist's ability to duplicate or create a landscape or human figure, a task which requires a rare level of hand-eye or sensory-motor integration. Differentiating a *b* from a *d* can be a visual observation or an auditory one, depending on whether the letters are written or spoken. We have many ways of observing, but academic learning depends most on vision, hearing, and the tactile-kinesthetic (touch and body awareness) senses. When any one of these is inefficient, all concept development suffers. Remember the varying versions of "elephant" held by the blind men who had felt only part of the huge beast? Similarly, a blind child can develop a fairly accurate concept of those things that he or she can hear or feel, but distance concepts such as clouds or purely visual concepts such as color must remain verbalizations. Concepts that are memorized but not meaningful remain at the same level for children whose senses are intact.

Finding the one that's different, listening for all of the sounds that the children can hear in the classroom or beyond, or tasting the difference between sweet and sour are examples of common activities in primary classrooms. Older students should be reacquainted with their sensory abilities. The rose lover, the gourmet cook, the perfectly pitched musician, and the tightwire walker are examples of persons who have developed one or more of their senses to a fine degree.

Classifying

Classification is a major building block skill in information processing (Beyer, 1987). The primary child may find all the ones that are red, are square, or can talk. We can ask older children to divide certain land masses into islands, isthmuses, and peninsulas, or to divide countries into democracies and nondemocracies (examples and nonexamples). An interesting activitiy is to ask a group of adults to define the concept of "family" by dividing a number of possible groupings of people into examples and nonexamples. Given the complexity of the modern family, this activity always reinforces the need to pay careful attention to alternatives when using classification as a concept-building exercise.

Critical Thinking

Ennis (1987) defined critical thinking as "reasonable reflective thinking that is focused on deciding what to believe or do" (p. 10). *Critical thinking,* in his opinion, is preferable to such terms as *higher-order thinking skills* (too vague), *reasoning* (too narrow), and *formal logic* (too difficult to infuse into other subject matter). He proposed that the subskills of critical thinking could be taught in a college-level course or taught sequentially throughout the elementary and secondary curriculum. Critical thinking skills are evaluative in nature. Ennis (1987) described the basic areas of critical thinking as clarity (focusing on the question, analyzing arguments, and asking questions), basis (judging credibility and observing), inference (inducing, deducing, and making value judgments), and interacting with others while practicing these skills.

Making inferences can serve as a good example of a critical thinking skill. Inferring may be defined as using observations to predict outcomes. A child who is told that he or she will be punished for fighting with a sibling and receives no punishment upon doing so will soon infer that a parental threat can be taken lightly. Prejudice evolves from the overgeneralization of inferences. (E.g., all New Yorkers are rude, all Californians are beach bums, or all midwesterners are unsophisticated hicks.)

An extension of studying inference is the process of distinguishing what is factual from what is inferred. Stating that George Washington was our first president is factual. Assuming that Washington enjoyed the presidency as evidenced by the fact that he served two terms is unsupported inference. Unfortunately, much of our knowledge of history may be distorted because we must rely upon the observations of others. There is a high probability that some of what we read may be historians' inferences rather than actual observations. (This, too, is an inference.) Each time the phrases "may be" or "probably" or "it seems to me" appear in this book, you are reading an inference by this writer. While this certainly leaves room for honest disagreement, inferences do move knowledge forward in small, although occasionally inaccurate steps.

A major emphasis of critical thinking is on the ability to recognize factual, relevant, nonprejudicial information as it is interspersed among all other input that we receive. The persistence of the "reappearance of Elvis" myth, the content of the supermarket tabloids and radio and television talk shows, and much of the rhetoric of political campaigns would not persist if we were truly a critically thinking society. Just as we have to recognize bias and illogicality in others, we need even more to recognize it in ourselves. One would like to think, to paraphrase Churchill, that "my only prejudice is against prejudice itself"; however, personal biases surround us and guide more of our behavior than we would like to admit. The key to critical thinking is to be aware that, since these human fallacies exist, we need to be vigilant in limiting their impact upon us.

The practical application of critical thinking in a classroom comes from systematically teaching children to ask questions that will elicit information that can lead to critically derived conclusions. Such questions might include the following:

- How is x like y? How are they different?
- What do you mean by _____?
- Is your favorite sports star a *real* expert on the product he or she sells? Why, then, do you suppose he or she does that commercial?
- Do you believe that the history books are accurate? Why are the contributions of white males more prevalent in these books than those of women or minorities?
- Compare a new history book with one that is 30 years old. Has the content changed in the discussion of the same events? Why?
- When you tell your mom that *everyone* is going to the mall, what are your assumptions (or your credibility, or your logic)?

Teaching critical thinking to children can be done through the study of advertising, through putting doubt into their acceptance of the neutrality and complete honesty of various media, or through comparing and contrasting the same story reported in a "conservative" and a "liberal" paper or newscast. Teachers might also encourage the discussion of letters to the editor that follow a major report on a volatile issue such as abortion, crime, or drugs in the schools. The topics for critical thinking are all around us. We must take responsibility for presenting both the topics and the ways in which children can develop evaluative criteria for judging the opinions of others and for forming their own.

Other Thinking Skills

Beyer (1987) used the term *micro-thinking* to identify additional cognitive skills. The most common example of microthinking skills is Bloom's *Taxonomy of Cognitive Educational Objectives*(1956). Most teachers in training are introduced to this system. Gifted educators have used the taxonomy as one of the basic ways to structure curriculum for bright students. In this writer's experience, most new graduate students in gifted education recognize the taxonomy, but few can use it effectively without further instruction and practice. This observation underscores the need to move beyond the basic knowledge level (learning of facts) even in graduate education.

Bloom's taxonomy may be described as having two levels. The lower level is comprised of knowledge, comprehension, and application. The upper level consists of analysis, synthesis, and evaluation. The lower level can be envisioned as steps in a process, each building on the other. The upper level can be envisioned as three processes of equal importance.

A personal experience will illustrate the use of the taxonomy. To demonstrate for their teachers how to teach thinking, a questioning sequence was presented to 12 different groups of kindergarten students. Time was limited to 15 minutes per class, and the taxonomy was chosen as the basis for the lesson because it was assumed that the teachers would recognize it. Each of the 12 heterogeneous groups of children was able to enter into a good discussion in this short amount of time. In the following list, abbreviated definitions of the taxonomy are linked to the questions asked and answers received during this teaching exercise.

1. *Knowledge. Acquiring and recalling facts.* This level can be the equivalent to the "garbage in, garbage out" (GIGO) of computer language, with little thought processing in the middle. Memorization, not understanding, is the basis for this level.

   Example: "What are some of the things you remember that were in *Goldilocks and the Three Bears*?" (This type of question is useful for introducing a lesson, reviewing the previous day's lesson, or double checking an assumed knowledge base.)

   Each group of children was able to name Goldilocks, the bears, chairs, beds, and porridge (presumed by some to be soup and by others to be oatmeal). In addition, some were sure a wolf was involved, raising the necessity for differentiating between Goldilocks and Red Riding Hood.

2. *Comprehension. This level adds understanding to recall.* Meaningful education begins at this level.

   Example: "Why did Goldilocks' parents give her that name?"

   (This question demonstrates the leap from recall to some understanding of the significance of the label.) Each group was able to discern the significance of both "gold" and "locks," but some children were puzzled by the discussion. Further examples and clarification would have been appropriate if more time had been available.

3. *Application. Using what is understood in a real or simulated situation; replicating or generalizing.* Much of what happens in classrooms can be considered application activities. Thought problems in mathematics or comprehension activities in lan-

guage arts give children an opportunity to practice and apply what they have learned. Bridging the gap between school simulations and real-life uses is more difficult.

Example: "What would have been a good name for Goldilocks if she had had brown hair?"

One child was convinced that "Natalie" would have been the perfect choice. A number of children, however, indicated their ability to generalize and apply the concept by suggesting "Chocolatelocks" or "Brownilocks." Had they only memorized the knowledge that this was the girl's name, but not understood its significance, they could not have made this application.

4. *Analysis. Using data; gathering information to form a conclusion.*

Analysis forms the basis of research and scientific inquiry.

Example: "Why do you think Goldilocks was in the woods in the first place?"

This is not a pure analysis question because the answer had to be inferred by the children. Such responses as "She was taking a walk and got lost," "She was looking for flowers and butterflies," or "Her mother had told her to get out of the house" showed a good analytic approach to the possible reasons for her arrival at the bears' home.

5. *Synthesis. Creating something new by using or recombining previously learned knowledge and experience in a different way.* This is the creative process we see in children's writing, art work, or science fair exhibits. Innovative adults are synthesizers regardless of the discipline they represent. Most inventive ideas are based firmly in the work of those who have preceded them.

Example: "Tell me a story about what might have happened had the bears not let Goldilocks out of the house" or "What if the bears had visited Goldilocks rather than the other way around?"

Time prohibited the children from responding in great detail. Had it occurred, the creative answers should have reflected an *analysis* of the situation, *comprehension* of the conflict involved, and *application* of that comprehension in a way that was unique to the imagination of the individual child.

6. *Evaluation. Judging one's own or other's behavior or products.* We often equate evaluation with grading. Its best use, and the one we must teach children, is monitoring the process of creation until the final product has been completed. This can be accomplished by providing feedback to oneself or others as the process progresses and by judging the final product in terms of what was done well and what could be improved. This is far preferable to equating success or failure to a single letter grade. Unfortunately, the grading process often stresses what the teacher values rather than helping to develop the evaluative capabilities of the child.

Example: "Was Goldilocks a good girl or a naughty girl? Tell me a way in which she was good or naughty."

Examples of Goldilocks as a naughty girl were easy to elicit. A few children were able to point to such good traits as her politeness in knocking at the door before she went in or her original intent (in their version) to simply take a walk and look at the flowers and butterflies.

Many commercial materials now exist that are based on the taxonomy. The publishers listed in Appendix A are good resources for such material. Readers interested in using the taxonomy with crossover children (or others) are encouraged to put themselves on the mailing lists of these excellent sources.

Inductive, Deductive, and Analogic Reasoning

The use of the taxonomy can be enhanced if students have good reasoning skills. Students who can induce are able to generalize from specifics; those who deduce can move from generalizations to specifics; those who think analogically can use parallel information to provide meaning.

Inductive reasoning can be very personal or it can be an enjoyable small-group activity. Beyer (1987) suggested an activity in which a list of words common during colonial times is presented to a social studies class. The students are asked to classify these words in any way that they wish, then abstract from the classifications some basic information about that period of history. An important step in this process is to give the different groups time to share the ways in which they completed the task.

The classic syllogism is a structured and enjoyable way of teaching *deduction.* For example:

All Ohioans are known as Buckeyes.

I was born in Ohio and have lived here all of my life.

Therefore, I am a Buckeye.

This format can be used with any content. Gifted children may enjoy the "game" of fitting a rule or concept into this format. The repetitive structure of the form may benefit the children with learning disabilities by facilitating storage and retrieval of the information.

Analogies are thinking tasks that incorporate recall, inference, and relationship (Sternberg, 1984). For example:

A circle is to an oblong as a square is to a _____.

Love is to hate as hot is to _____.

William Shakespeare is to Hamlet as Louisa May Alcott is to _____.

These examples illustrate the ease with which analogies can be incorporated into any content area. Midwestern Publications has a number of workbooks that provide good practice in inductive, deductive, and analogic thinking as well as many of the other critical thinking skills described previously.

PUBLISHED PROGRAMS FOR TEACHING THINKING

Books on teaching thinking tend to take one of two approaches. One is to describe a particular program intended to be used in a separate time slot in the curriculum. The other tends to discuss individual skills that can be practiced within the existing curriculum. With proper development, either approach can be generalized to real-life thinking situations. Both are useful. The reality of teaching is that few extra minutes exist, so that ideas easily incorporated into existing content may be more widely accepted. On the other hand, the intensity of practice provided by the specialized material will illustrate the ability to enhance thinking through a definable set of skills.

Two popular programs for teaching thinking are the CoRT thinking materials of deBono (1986) and a series of books known collectively as *Philosophy for Children* (Lipman, 1978, 1980, 1981, 1982a, 1982b, 1983). Each of these programs offers an introduction to and guided practice in a number of skills, is well written, and is an excellent resource for novice teachers of thinking skills. The disadvantages are the time necessarily taken from other curricular content, the necessity to buy additional material, and the issue of transferring skills to other material.

deBono's CoRT materials are published in a series of work cards that provide common applications of the skills his program aims to develop. In his words, the goal of thinking lessons should be a self-image not of "I am intelligent," but of "I am a thinker." According to deBono, intelligence is a value image that has to be defended, while thinking is an operational image that demands action (deBono, 1985, p. 9). The CoRT program consists of six 10-lesson sets. An example of a basic skill is determining the **p**lusses, **m**inuses, and **i**nteresting elements (PMI) of a given problem. deBono described PMI as an attention-getting device that helps us to rapidly scan the many aspects inherent in most decision-making situations. For instance, if we were to propose 3 months of school and 9 months of vacation for each school year, many students (and teachers) would consider this to be a grand idea. However, a quick PMI might bring out such points as boredom after too much vacation, the problems of childcare for working parents, the need to learn certain material before college, and the possibility that entrance to college would be delayed by the shorter year. We would also be having vacation in different kinds of weather than we now anticipate. In a very few minutes, most children or adults can state a lot of knowledge and/or opinions about any subject. A more focused discussion can follow. Note the similarity between PMI and the fact-finding step of the creative problem-solving model described previously.

Lateral thinking is deBono's term for the style of creative thinking for which he considers the term creativity to be an inadequate label. His description of the process is "pattern switching within a patterned system" (1985, p. 85). By this, he means examining issues from varied angles. He considers lateral thinking to be more neutral than creativity because examination may sometimes come up with nothing; or it may produce a new and better solution to an old problem. Other deBono techniques have equally sound rationales and applications. They are described in the book *deBono's Thinking Course,* as well as in the separately published CoRT system.

Philosophy for Children originated at the Institute for the Advancement of Philosophy for Children, Montclair State College, New Jersey, under the direction of Matthew Lipman. The program consists of story books that are now available for students in kindergarten through early high school. Lipman described the manuals as "crammed with exercises and discussion plans keyed to the concepts and skills in the novels" (1987, p. 153). These concepts include the principles of logic, reasoning skills, ethical reasoning, and moral practice. Lipman acknowledged that the program can be used as an innovative way to teach thinking skills; but he preferred to envision the series as a guide for developing the classroom into a community of inquiry that will use Aristotelian logic, scientific inquiry, and Socratic dialogue. Training is required to become proficient in using this program. Trainers from the Institute will come on-site to train teachers. Follow-up is provided, including in-class teaching demonstrations and critiques of the participating teachers' own teaching.

The thoroughness of the materials and the training package make it more expensive than many other systems, but the follow-up sessions make actual use of the techniques more likely.

Although many gifted classrooms use the CoRt or *Philosophy for Children* programs, they do not appear to be in use in any learning disability programs. These materials are a good example of techniques that can be incorporated into special education or inclusion programs for the benefit of crossover children and other students with learning disabilities.

TECHNOLOGY AND THINKING

The technological explosion of the last few years and the rapid move toward inclusion of computers in the classroom has provided children with access to an exciting avenue of exploration of thinking skills and creativity. Unfortunately, drill and practice or playing computer games as a reward for completing work does little to enhance either thinking or creativity. However, for teachers willing to explore additional options, activities specifically designed for enrichment are available.

Barr (1990) proposed five goals for enhancing learning through technology: enhancing independent learning; individualizing learning; and making learning more interactive, more interdisciplinary, and more intuitive. Howell (1994) elaborated upon these five goals with the following suggestions:

- *Independent learning.* Technology enhances independent learning through using electronic databases, accessing mass storage devices such as CD-ROM, manipulating statistical data through appropriate software programs, and integrating text and graphics through word processing.

- *Individualized learning.* The variety of applications now available gives students and teachers opportunities to accommodate various student learning styles. Multimedia-based presentations allow for the creation or presentation of programs with unlimited variations.

- *Interactive learning.* New systems provide telecommunication networks, access to experts, feedback, and collaboration with others.

- *Interdisciplinary learning.* The communication capabilities of the new technology allow access to the databases of multiple disciplines, facilitate communication among novices and experts at various sites, and provide simulated and actual practice in real-world problems.

- *Intuitive learning.* Visualization techniques such as virtual reality, simulations, and artificial intelligence systems open up possibilities for creative, unintended learning.

People born before the Computer Age may continue to struggle with these mind-boggling possibilities, but they are, or should be, the reality of today's children. It is important to seek out experts who are aware of existing options and can help adapt them to the needs of a particular child.

THE INTEGRATIVE EDUCATION MODEL

The many techniques just described do not constitute a total enrichment program. This chapter concludes with a model that describes the type of program into which these various techniques could readily fit. Barbara Clark, a major contributor to the field of gifted education, spent several years deriving the Integrative Education model from her study of brain/mind research conducted in several disciplines and from application of her hypotheses in the New Age School in Los Angeles. The model is meant as a blueprint for restructuring education for all children. In brief, Integrative Education "combines thinking with feeling, the senses, and intuition. Through this model each function of the brain is allowed to support the others, resulting in a very coherent, powerful learning experience" (Clark, 1986, p. 27). Clark identified seven key components in the model and, while noting that many can be administered separately, suggested that the most powerful outcome will occur when all components are being used. They include:

- *A responsive environment* that is based on mutual respect, cooperative planning, a workshop atmosphere, a flexible curriculum, an emphasis on individual and small-group lessons, and the inclusion of the student as an active participant in the learning process. The learner both self-monitors progress and is monitored by assessment, contracting, and evaluation.

- *Relaxation and tension reduction* through the use of such techniques as progressive relaxation or the use of calming music or colors to provide a relaxing learning environment. While this may seem far afield from "education," many special education teachers start their students' days with a low-level transition activity such as a puzzle or game. Some play calming music for the same purpose. Students may endure long and tiring bus rides before they get to school, may have to get themselves ready for school, and/or they may have to endure a chaotic morning at home before they leave for school. The mind has a limited supply of energy which, if used up by unresolved tension, will be unavailable for the critical tasks of learning. A 5- to 10-minute relaxation activity may free the harried brain for many more minutes of productive activity.

- *Movement and physical encoding* is the "I do and I understand" of Confucius. Clark suggests that learning is enhanced by the use of role plays, simulations, and the physical manipulation of materials. The former are widely used in gifted education; the latter, more typically in special education. Clark's suggestions certainly "cross over" the two.

- *Empowering language and behavior* reinforces the use of the strategy approach described previously. When confronted by "I can't" or "I don't know how to do it," Clark suggests countering with "What are some of the possibilities?" rather than an immediate adult demonstration or solution to the problem. Empowerment implies emotional as well as cognitive supportiveness.

- *Choice and perceived control* are included as a key concept based on Clark's review of the literature, which links student achievement and positive self-concept to the perception of personal choice and control. When comparing the approaches used in gifted and special education, one of the intriguing questions is the irrationality of freely giving choice and control to gifted children (at least in gifted resource rooms), while rigidly structuring the classrooms of most children in special education. If we concur with Clark's conclusion that good decision making is based upon multiple opportunities and guided practice, we must seek ways to expand opportunities for regular class children and those with disabilities to practice these skills.

- *Complex and challenging cognitive activity* is, according to Clark, necessary for making all parts of the brain function. Without relating cognition to sensing, feeling, and intuition, it remains meaningless and is soon forgotten. Recall, if you will, the "crammed" and now forgotten history dates or mathematical formulas of your own schooling. On the other hand, we cannot underestimate the need for the development of a basic knowledge base. Clark's admonition here is that the knowledge base will be lost unless it is applied in a complex and meaningful context.

- *Intuition and integration,* like relaxation, may seem out of place in some classrooms. While the acceptance of intuition as a universal trait may be difficult for some, a preponderance of "intuitive" types as measured by personality type instruments has been found in gifted and crossover populations (Bireley & Hoehn, 1988; Piirto, 1994). Intuitive respondents consistently select items that stress ideas, orientation to the future, and integration of concepts. These are the very traits that Clark described in her discussion of this key concept.

The components of Clark's (1986) model integrate most of the needs of the crossover child. Anyone involved in the development of a program specifically for crossover children should read her entire book.

SUMMARY

This chapter described a variety of strategies for differentiating curriculum and assisting children to develop the component skills of thinking. The importance of knowing, teaching, and practicing skills such as creative thinking, critical thinking, and higher-order thinking was discussed. While crossover children often break down in the acquisition of certain basic academic subjects, their ability to think may not be impaired. It is important that their disability does not prevent them from being exposed to the opportunity to learn and use thinking skills.

References

Barr, D. (1990). A solution in search of a problem: The role of technology in educational reform. *Journal for the Education of the Gifted, 1,* 79–95.

Beyer, B. (1987). *Practical strategies for the teaching of thinking.* Boston: Allyn & Bacon.

Bireley, M., & Hoehn, L. (1988). Mental processing in gifted children. *Journal of the Illinois Council of the Gifted, 7,* 28–31.

Bloom, B. (Ed.). (1956). *Taxonomy of education objectives. Handbook I: Cognitive domain.* New York: David McKay.

Clark, B. (1986). *Optimizing learning: The integrative education model in the classroom.* Columbus, OH: Merrill.

deBono, E. (1985). *deBono's thinking course.* New York: Facts on File.

deBono, E. (1986). *CoRT thinking program.* Elmsford, NY: Pergamon.

Eberle, B. (1971). *SCAMPER.* Buffalo, NY: D.O.K.

Eberle, B. (1982). *Visual thinking.* Buffalo, NY: D.O.K.

Eberle, B., & Stanish, B. (1985). *CPS for kids: A resource book for teaching creative problem-solving to children.* Buffalo, NY: D.O.K.

Ennis, R. (1987). A taxonomy of critical thinking dispositions and abilities. In J. Baron & R. Sternberg (Eds.), *Teaching thinking skills: Theory and practice* (pp.9–26). New York: Freeman.

Howell, R. (1994). Technological innovations in the education of gifted and talented students. In J. Genshaft, M. Bireley, & C. Hollinger (Eds.), *Serving gifted and talented students: A resource for school personnel* (pp. 155–171). Austin, TX: Pro-Ed.

Kupferberg, H. (1986). *Amadeus: A Mozart mosaic.* New York: McGraw-Hill.

Lipman, M. (1978). *Suki.* Upper Montclair, NJ: First Mountain Foundation.

Lipman, M. (1980). *Mark.* Upper Montclair, NJ: First Mountain Foundation.

Lipman, M. (1981). *Pixie.* Upper Montclair, NJ: First Mountain Foundation.

Lipman, M. (1982a). *Harry Stottlemeier's discovery.* Upper Montclair, NJ: First Mountain Foundation.

Lipman, M. (1982b). *Kio and Gus.* Upper Montclair, NJ: First Mountain Foundation.

Lipman, M. (1983). *Lisa.* Upper Montclair, NJ: First Mountain Foundation.

Lipman, M. (1987). Some thoughts on the the foundations of reflective education. In J. Baron & R. Sternberg (Eds.), *Teaching thinking skills: Theory and practice* (pp. 151–161). New York: Freeman.

Noller, R. (1977). *Scratching the surface of creative problem solving: A bird's eye view of CPS.* Buffalo, NY: D.O.K.

Osborn, A. (1963). *Applied imagination* (3rd ed.). New York: Scribners.

Piirto, J. (1994). *Talented children and adults: Their development and education.* New York: Merrill.

Sanders, D., & Sanders, J. (1984). *Teaching creativity through metaphor: An integrated brain approach.* New York: Longman.

Sternberg, R. (1984). How can we teach intelligence? *Educational Leadership, 42*: 40.

Treffinger, D. (1990, April). *Rethinking creativity.* Paper presented at the meeting of the Ohio Association for Gifted Children, Columbus.

VanTassel-Baska, J. (1989). Appropriate curriculum for the gifted. In J. Feldhusen, J. VanTassel-Baska, & K. Seeley (Eds.), *Excellence in educating the gifted* (pp.175–192). Denver: Love.

6

Crossover Children Grow Up

I know he wants to go to college. He's so slow in getting his work done. I'm not sure he can handle a full load.

I want to be an archaeologist, not a secretary. They have to let me take college prep courses!

The most helpful thing I found was that there was a place where someone understood what I needed and didn't laugh at me and helped me get what I needed.

My mom spent twelve years telling people I'm not retarded. I've screwed up a few times here, but I've learned what I should have learned in high school. In high school, they didn't want me in composition. They told me I should grease tractors.

Crossover children become adolescents, then adults. The services available to exceptional children are not yet equaled by services available for them in their later years. Recent legislation and militancy on the part of adults with learning disabilities are changing both our awareness and our legal obligation, but interest in older persons with disabilities still needs to become a greater public priority. Some crossover children may enter maturity with little need for supportive services; others may need occasional lifelong assistance. Even those who have overcome the major academic deficiencies of childhood may run into residual weaknesses that may cause difficulties at unexpected moments.

The professional community concerned with learning disabilities has begun to address the needs of adolescents and adults with learning disabilities, especially the need for a good transition from high school to postsecondary employment or education. Patton and Polloway (1992) surveyed two major journals and found that articles on adults with disabilities were scarce in the late 1970's but, by 1990, 13% of the articles in the *Journal of Learning Disabilities* and 28% of those in the *Learning Disabilities Quarterly* dealt with the subject. Many of the studies discussed the characteristics of adults with learning disabilities, how they differ from their nondisabled peers, and the transition skills and institutional accommodations necessary if they are to become economically successful and emotionally secure.

VULNERABILITIES OF THE CROSSOVER ADOLESCENT

Needs Related to Learning Disability

Huntington and Bender (1993) reviewed all data-based research on adolescents with learning disabilities over a 9-year period. They were mainly concerned with five areas of emotional well-being: self-concept, attribution of control, anxiety, depression, and suicide. The academic self-concept of adolescents with learning disabilities clearly is poor, compared to that of their nondisabled peers. General self-concept studies have been more equivocal, but they do tend to indicate a less positive self-concept in the group with learning disabilities. The adolescents with learning disabilities tend to attribute both success and failure to internal rather than external causes, a sign of fairly severe self-criticism. Those who did attribute failure to external causes appeared to make better academic gains and behave more appropriately in secondary classrooms.

Adolescents with learning disabilities appear to have significantly higher levels of trait (long-term) anxiety than their nondisabled peers and have more sleep problems and somatic complaints. Likewise, the studies reviewed revealed that depression occurs in higher levels and to a more severe degree in children and adolescents with learning disabilities than in their nondisabled peers. The studies indicated that about one-fifth of this population suffer from some degree of depression. Suicide also appears to be more prevalent, although fewer studies have addressed this issue. Huntington and Bender suggested that cognitive deficits that occur with learning disability limit the individual's ability to generate alternative solutions to stressful situations, resulting in a helplessness that may lead to suicide.

Stone and La Greca (1990) studied a multiracial group of 547 intermediate school students including 57 who were mainstreamed students with learning disabilities. From sociometric data, they found that the group with learning disabilities tended to be disliked more often than their nondisabled peers. Students with disabilities who were aggressive and disruptive tended to be rejected by peers; those who were shy and withdrawn were likely to be neglected and to experience social anxiety. Stone and La Greca (1990) cited numerous studies that supported their findings, a few that detected no social status difficulties in groups with disabilities, and none that attributed a higher social status to those subjects. Most of the studies were conducted on elementary school populations, but, as Huntington and Bender (1993) found, the social and emotional issues related to learning disability are likely to remain and perhaps become exaggerated during the adolescent years.

All adolescents must struggle with physiological changes and sexual awakening as well as the urge for independence from parents and the corresponding need for identification with the peer group. Further, they must develop a personal value system, and use of that system in the choice of career and lifestyle. If childhood social experiences have been inadequate and coping strategies have not been taught or developed, the adolescent with an unresolved learning disability may have a particularly difficult time in establishing a positive thrust toward adulthood.

The worst case scenario is that the adolescent with learning disabilities may be drawn into lawbreaking. There has been a longstanding debate about the relationship of learning disability and juvenile delinquency. Brier (1989), in his review of the literature on this topic, noted that much of the research has used imprecise definitions of "learning disability." These studies have placed the percentage of incarcerated youth with learning disability at anywhere from 12% to over 70%. In spite of methodological problems, Brier concluded that "the presence of a learning disability does seem to place a youngster at increased risk of a delinquent outcome" (p. 546). There are several possible reasons suggested for this relationship, including the following:

- Difficulties with impulse control and attention (associated with ADHD).

- Problems with conceptualization, comprehension, and judgment (associated with language deficits and verbally mediated self-regulation deficits).

- Problems with social perception (associated with poor interpretation of the nonverbal gestures and expressions of others). Larson (1988) generalized this to a more pervasive social-cognitive problem-solving deficit.

- Problems with school failure and dropping out related to problems of self-image and frustration.

- Differential treatment by the court systems (possibly associated with an inability to make behavior more appropriate for interaction with court personnel).

Brier (1989) did note that low average IQs and dysfunctional families are two critical factors in addition to the characteristics just listed. This could lead to the conclusion that the intelligence of the crossover child lowers the risk of a delinquent outcome. However, each of the problems listed here has been discussed elsewhere in this book as a potential problem for the crossover child. One must conclude that, when any of the cited deficits exists, academic and behavioral intervention is critical regardless of IQ. Even if these deficits do not lead to lawbreaking, they threaten the adolescent's ability to establish a mentally healthy adulthood.

Needs Related to Giftedness

It might be hoped or assumed that the giftedness of crossover adolescents would help them cope with problems associated with their disabilities. While, with appropriate instruction, the problem-solving skills of the crossover adolescent are likely to exceed those of less able peers, giftedness carries its own emotional dangers. Being different, regardless of *how* one is different, becomes increasingly more important in the mind of the peer-oriented adolescent. Therefore, while the gifted as a group tend to be socially and emotionally healthy, certain factors make some individuals quite vulnerable. Janos (1994), based on his experience with accelerated college students, found that overemphasis on academics sometimes diminishes "wellness" in other areas—emotional, social, physical, occupational, or spiritual. He suggested that secondary and postsecondary schools must take responsibility for addressing the broader needs of gifted individuals by providing counseling and peer group discussion opportunities.

Frey (1991) related the emotional vulnerability of the gifted adolescent to a number of factors. She cited uneven development (developmental dysplasia), inadequate coping skills, perfectionism, a lack of risktaking, an inordinate desire to please parents and other significant adults, and a feeling of being different and isolated from peers as potential reasons for concern.

The effect of dysplasia on the crossover adolescent cannot be overemphasized. All bright children must cope with mental abilities that lead them where their motor or social development will not allow them to follow. Add to that mix the disparity of having certain disabilities that may hinder the achievement of age-appropriate academic or social behavior and the likelihood of isolation or rebellion may increase. Unfortunately, substance abuse, sexual experimentation, depression, and/or contemplation of suicide may become outlets for the troubled teen. In an article about adults with learning disabilities who are suicide prone, Kowalchuk and King (1989) suggested that a cognitive behavioral program that involves the adult in the remediation process should be used to prevent suicide. Ultimate success will come to those who can unload their "emotional baggage" (p.178), establish a belief that they *can* become effective, accept their limitations, give up their wish to be exactly like everyone else, and receive from others (or a significant other) an increased sense of self-worth. These steps would seem to generalize to crossover adolescents and to solving most emotional problems. Whatever the manifestation, educators and parents should be particularly vigilant in their support when a behavior change is noted in the crossover adolescent. They should not necessarily attribute it to "just a phase."

CAREER CHOICE AND POSTSECONDARY EDUCATION

Given the many vulnerabilities of the adolescent student, it appears logical to assume that emotional support and vocational counseling should be considered as important as academic programming. Identifying and providing appropriate transitional skills are important. Those skills should focus on personal responsibility and relationships, occupational selection and preparation, home and family, leisure time pursuits, community involvement, and emotional and physical health (Patton & Polloway, 1992). Additionally, the selection of an appropriate institution for students wishing to pursue postsecondary education is important.

Learning Style and Career Choice

Most of the decisions faced by the crossover adolescent are shared by all adolescents. Consequently, not every decision should be based on differences that exist between crossover groups and those of average ability. One helpful strategy in choosing a career is to look at the information that can be gained from a learning style or personal type inventory. Giving every student such an inventory in junior high school would be helpful in early career selection. A thorough interpretation of the results can play a significant role in determining high school programs and college majors, but they should not be used to discard options. Too many examples exist of motivation overcoming learning obstacles.

One good choice is the Myers-Briggs Type Indicator (MBTI) (Briggs & Myers, 1977), which has career counseling applications that are as important as those related to education. Considerable study has been completed on the relationships between career choice and the traits assessed by the MBTI. These relationships bear repeating (Myers & McCaulley, 1985):

- *Extraverts* (E) like variety and action in the workplace, like to have people around, are good communicators, and may be impatient with long, slow jobs or complicated procedures.

- *Introverts* (I) like a quiet, uninterrupted workplace, work contentedly alone, may not be good communicators, tend to be good detail people, and can maintain interest in one project for a long time.

- *Sensers* (S) like an established order of doing things, like using learned skills rather than learning new ones, are patient with details and good with facts, and use a step-by-step process to reach conclusions.

- *Intuiters* (N) like new ideas and procedures, seek variety and complicated situations, and are imprecise and error prone with factual material.

- *Thinkers* (T) are unemotional or cold in dealing with people, analytic, impersonal, fair, and firm-minded.

- *Feelers* (F) are "people-pleasers," are aware of others' feelings, are sympathetic, like harmony, and need praise.

- *Judgers* (J) like to plan ahead and stick to the plan, dislike interruptions or new things not in the plan, and like to finish one thing before starting another.

- *Perceivers* (P) are curious and like new situations—leading to the lack of conclusion of one project before others are begun—may have difficulty making decisions, and may put off unpleasant tasks.

It is easy to see how some of these general characteristics become important in the workplace. When they are combined into types (e.g., INFP, ESTJ), even more precise assumptions can be made about the match between the individual and a certain career choice. It should be noted that each of the 16 possible types has occurred in every profession studied, but that predictable skewing occurs. For instance, psychologists are overwhelmingly intuitive, but rather evenly split on the other dimensions. Small-business managers are most frequently STJs. Intuiters and perceivers who have clerical and mechanical jobs that require routine and precision tend to leave such positions much more frequently than sensers and judgers, who excel in these areas.

One way to resolve differences between a student's choice and the traits important in a given profession may be to look at specialties within that profession. Preschool and elementary teachers are most often SFJs and high school teachers are more likely to be STJs. The F/T difference clearly reflects the stereotypic people-versus-content orientation of these two groups. University professors tend to be more intuitive than sensing, reflecting a greater fascination with new ideas (research) than is true of their K–12 colleagues. The source of this information (Myers & McCaulley, 1985) contains the percentages of the various types found within many professions as well as other assistance in refining the career counseling and college selection process. Another source available is *Do What You Are: Discover the Perfect Career for You Through the Secrets of Personality Type* (Tieger & Barron-Tieger, 1992). The latter is less research oriented, but both are highly recommended resources.

POSTSECONDARY CHOICES

Section 504 of the Rehabilitation Act of 1973 and the Americans with Disabilities Act (ADA) mandate against discrimination against persons with disabilities in higher education institutions. They further mandate that appropriate academic adjustments be provided to allow meaningful access to the institution and programs within it. Accommodations for students with learning disabilities are more complex than removing physical barriers for those with visual or motor disabilities (Scott, 1994). Time extensions for test taking or substituting courses to circumvent serious specific learning deficits are much harder to understand, particularly when service providers have limited background in both the disability and the law.

In reviewing the law, Scott (1994) described the intention as providing equal access, not ensuring identical results. She suggested that appropriate modifications might include extending time for completion of requirements; allowing course substitutions; conducting courses in different ways; evaluating in ways that assess achievement, not the disability; providing taped texts; and allowing tape recorders in the classroom. Whether or not an accommodation is reasonable will ultimately be determined by the courts. Scott (1994) concluded that accommodations should provide as integrated an experience as possible, but they should do so without compromising the essential requirements of a specific program. Further, they should not pose an appreciable threat to personal or public safety and should not impose undue financial or administrative burdens on an institution.

Four-Year Colleges and Universities

Much of this book has been based on the author's study of elementary and junior high students from the late 1980s to the present, as well as earlier experience gained from helping to found and working in the program for college students with learning disabilities at Wright State University. The students in this program did not, as a group, test as high in intelligence as the crossover children, but some were clearly gifted as well as having learning disabilities. The many insights gained from working with the university group, as well as recent studies cited in the literature, have been used to predict the needs of crossover individuals in high school, postsecondary education, and adulthood.

In the early 1970s, few high school programs existed for students with learning disabilities. Such students were, for the most part, placed in regular classes in a "sink or swim" mode. Few were encouraged to take college preparatory courses. Many were discouraged from this track even when they requested it. It was in this atmosphere that the Wright State program began as a pilot program. Discussions began at the prompting of a graduate student who was a mother of two students with learning disabilities and president of the Ohio Association for Children with Learning Disabilities (now OLDA). In the latter capacity, she had received several letters from young adults who were frustrated in their attempts to compete successfully in college in spite of their own belief that they had good basic intelligence.

Following many brainstorming sessions and meetings, permission was received to start the pilot program. In many ways, it was an ideal setting for such an experiment. As a new university, the campus was totally accessible and was gaining a national reputation as a site for education of students with physical disabilities. An Office of Handicapped Student Services with specifically trained counselors was in place, and such services as taped textbooks, tutoring, developmental reading and writing, and test proctoring were provided for these students. Permission was given by the director to make use of the existing services. The outcome of this study is reported elsewhere in some detail (Bireley & Manley, 1980; Bireley, Landers, Schlaerth, & Vernooy, 1986). From an initial group of 3 students, the program has grown to an annual enrollment of about 150 students. Nationwide, services for students with both learning and physical disabilities are now typical on campuses that receive federal funding. A number of colleges cater specifically to individuals with special needs.

Some of the lessons learned from the Wright State experience seem applicable to crossover children. Decisions that will affect readiness for postsecondary schooling need to be made prior to entrance into high school. One such decision is the selection of a high school academic program that will prepare the student for college. Several roadblocks may interfere with the uneventful selection of a college preparatory course. These roadblocks must be acknowledged and faced squarely by the crossover child, parents, counselors, and teachers. Unfortunately, a professional who aids in the decision-making process may not have a good background in learning disabilities, and most students and parents are not aware of how critical a decision at an early age can be. The following factors should be considered by crossover children and their adult advocates before high school:

- *Crossover children may not be perceived as "college material,"* especially if they have been served in a program for students with learning disabilities for several years. Some school personnel will be prejudiced against enrolling such students into college prepatory courses. This type of prejudice will have to be faced head on by crossover students and their families. Facts supportive of ability should be kept in a family portfolio as well as in the school's cumulative records. If, as suggested throughout this book, both ability and disability have been recognized, problems of this nature are less likely to occur than if the entire educational emphasis has been on the child's disability.

- *Crossover children who have been served in LD resource rooms may not have an adequate knowledge base compared to other college preparatory students.* Resource rooms are designed to increase basic skill achievement and/or to control attentional or behavioral difficulties. Decreasing LD services and increasing regular class attendance (preferably full inclusion) should be accomplished by late elementary school for crossover children wishing to attend college. This is not to say that all support services should be discontinued, but that adequate opportunities for participation in content classes should be part of the master plan for such students.

- *Crossover children with residual skills deficits may find it difficult to keep up with the pace of the college preparatory classes.* Since the most common residual difficulty is in written language, a wide discrepancy in written work may exist between the crossover child and the typical college prepatory student. Understanding parents and teachers, supportive counselors, and permission to use technological aids are critical ingredients in overcoming the difficulties raised by the typical poor spelling and illegible handwriting of the crossover student.

  Additionally, the adolescent need to appear "normal" to the peer group cannot be overrated as an impediment to success at this time. While younger students and young adults may have little difficulty in asking others to take notes or copy assignments, the typical young adolescent would "rather die" than admit to such a need. Adults who aid adolescents with learning disabilities must be willing to engage in coverups of the disability while simultaneously helping the adolescents to confront and live with their weaknesses. It is a precarious journey for all concerned.

- *Depending upon the nature of the disability and the academic subjects it makes more difficult, there may be content areas in which some crossover students cannot achieve at an advanced level.* When the Wright State program was first started, the general curriculum (first 2 years) contained a number of choices that varied from major to major. Students with disabilities in math could avoid all but the most elementary of courses in this area, and similar adjustments could be made for different disability patterns. The national concern about the quality of education has tightened the requirements for both high school and college. Now students take more mathematics, more English, more science, and a foreign language in high school, or they must make up the deficits at the college level. At Wright State and many other universities, every student must complete a core curriculum that cuts across all discipline areas. While the intent of these requirements is good, the result may be to deny college success to some able crossover children with persistent deficiencies in a specific area. This problem is now being addressed on many campuses. For example, one compromise is to allow computer literacy or signing for the deaf as a substitute for a more traditional foreign language requirement.

- *Emotional stability and developing independence are as important to postsecondary success as are academic skills.* One of the earliest patterns detected in the Wright State program was the difference between students who had learned to cope with their disability and those who came to college still dependent upon their parents and lacking decision-making skills. During the initial interview, questions were addressed directly to the candidate. If the young person responded and seemed confident, the likelihood for success was great. On the other hand, it was a bad omen when the answers came from one of the parents and the student sat passively or reluctantly by while critical decisions were being made. The astute reader may be thinking that this is true of all entering college students. However, parents of children with disabilities are more likely than others to foster a condition termed *learned helplessness.* In our natural concern to protect our children from the cruelty of others and the problems they are likely to face, we may shelter them too much and fight their battles for much too long. The unfortunate consequence of this well-intentioned behavior is that the young adult develops a sense of loss of control over his or her own destiny, leading to a prolongation of dependency, anxiety, and a delay of social and emotional maturity (Sabatino, Miller, & Schmidt, 1981). Some special education teachers tend to duplicate parental behaviors in their attempt to advocate for children with special needs in the school system. For instance, Minskoff, Sautter, Sheldon, Steidle, and Baker (1988) concluded that, while the sheltered atmosphere of the high school special education class may lead to a more satisfactory secondary school experience, the student may not be receiving a helpful view of the real world in that setting. "In a relatively short time after completing high school, LD adults become more accurate in their self-perceptions and the reality of their situation. This sudden jolt into reality may result in LD adults feeling more frustrated and depressed" (Minskoff et al., p. 122).

Most crossover children will not be served in secondary LD classrooms. However, it is imperative that they, like children with more severe disabilities, be allowed to take gradual control of their lives. When necessary, specific instruction should be given in the ways in which they can do this. Behavioral self-control and problem solving are techniques that assist children to become captains of their own destinies. The importance of this philosophy cannot be overemphasized, as it relates to adult independence, competency, and success.

- *The initial career interest of the student may be impeded by the pattern of strengths and weaknesses of that individual.* For example, a student with disability in mathematics might find it most difficult to succeed in business, engineering, or certain science professions. A student with residual eye/hand disability cannot expect to become a commercial pilot, a professional athlete, or a surgeon. A student from several generations of attorneys may lack the language skills to join the family business. On the other hand, the strong hereditary link observed in the clinical studies of the crossover condition may make the professions of some parents ideal for their children.

  Supportive counseling may be needed when these difficult choices are being faced. Reality testing is important—for example, interviewing professionals concerning the demands of their daily schedule or, even better, "job shadowing" them during their daily routines. Once interest in an area has been established, families need to look at the college requirements for this choice, preferably during junior high school. Many students come to a university firmly committed to a certain major but with little idea of the specific requirements of that program. Muddling through the career decision-making process may work for gifted students, who can make up for deficiencies with relative ease. It may spell disaster for the crossover adolescent.

- *Choosing the right college will entail looking at many factors.* Size of the college, distance from home, "image," and cost are universal considerations. Crossover students must search for an institution that both challenges their ability and accommodates their learning differences and need for supportive services. Berger (1994) outlined the steps that gifted students, both achieving and underachieving, must take to find a suitable college setting. Mangrum and Strichart (1984) supplied a list of 18 questions that students who will need special services should ask about a potential program. These questions concern the availability of special admissions procedures, diagnostic testing, counselors with training in learning disabilities, course substitutions or special sections for students with disabilities, and specific special services such as notetakers or taped textbooks. Michael (1987) added that inquiry should be made about access to typists, computers, faculty members willing to act as resource persons, study and support groups, and guidance in college living. Using these resources as a guide, the crossover student should be able to develop a personal checklist of desires, steps to follow, and questions to ask when searching for an appropriate college setting.

High school teachers and counselors who serve gifted children, children with disabilities, and crossover children should have the Berger and the Mangrum and Strichart books in their professional libraries. The former provides a discussion of the unique needs of the gifted student, specific steps in student/college matching, and ways for students to present themselves effectively during the application and interviewing processes. The latter provides a comprehensive discussion of the issues faced by crossover children preparing for transition into college life. Good additional information is available in Nelson and Lignugaris/Kraft's (1989) review of articles that have been written on specific college programs. While crossover students may need limited supportive services at the college level, it is important to know whether or not that assistance is available at the institution of their choice.

Only one discussion was found that specifically dealt with crossover students and selective colleges. Shaywitz and Shaw (1988) reviewed the characteristics of this group, the criteria that should be used for admission, and the services that should be provided. Their discussion of admission criteria is a contribution not found in the other sources cited. They suggested using the following data sources to discover the crossover student with a good chance of being competitive in a selective university:

- High cognitive ability verified by an individual intelligence test and/or participation in various programs or experiences for gifted children.

- B grades in high school based on the understanding that these grades will underestimate a student's ability because of the frequent emphasis on neatness, inability to finish within time limits and so on.

- Scores into the 600s on untimed SATs.

- Personal qualities such as motivation, perseverance, and resiliency.

- The student's acceptance of the disability and any need for compensatory assistance, and the ability to organize time and balance study needs with extracurricular activities.

• *High school students with residual learning disability problems need to have specific instruction in the study skills needed in the college setting* (Mangrum & Strichart (1984). Postsecondary settings vary from high schools in a number of ways: Less time is spent in class; learning is more student centered and directed; and there is more freedom of choice and more emphasis on higher skill levels, long-term projects, and use of multiple reference sources (Brinckerhoff, Shaw, & McGuire, 1992). Dropping the requirement for term papers or exaggerated leniency in setting time limits will not provide the college-bound student with a reality check. Learning how to study differently for different subjects, using comprehension guides such as SQ3R, practicing time management, deciding which special services are necessary for personal survival, learning how to access these services, and continued emphasis on the development of deficient basic skills are necessary components of a successful secondary program for potential college students. Since many crossover children may not be enrolled in secondary LD programs per se, concerned counselors, special educators, and gifted educators may need to work together to deliver such content within the busy secondary schedule.

Alternatives to 4-year Colleges

Four-year college programs differ from 2-year and technical programs in that the former require "general" education in addition to training for a profession. The goal of the 4-year program is to graduate an educated person as well as a competent professional. No one would dispute this aim, especially those families who have a tradition of college education. However, it is the general education requirements that most often trip up the college student with learning disabilities. Many cannot overcome their basic skills deficiencies to the extent needed for college success. Good alternatives exist. Most of the programs in community colleges and technical schools provide immediate immersion in the skills of chosen programs. Many provide intensive developmental education services for the basic skills, but it is important to double check on specific institutions. The availability of other supportive services and understanding of the unique needs of the student with learning disabilities cannot be assumed. For instance, in an Ohio study (Snyder, Bireley, Jones, Marra, & Scholl, 1986), secondary LD teachers believed that nearly three-quarters of their students could be successful in some type of postsecondary education (42% in vocational/technical, 22% in 2-year community or junior colleges, and 10% in 4-year institutions). The respondents' pupils represented about one-fourth of Ohio secondary students with learning disabilities for that year. In a companion survey, respondents from 65, or 41%, of Ohio's postsecondary institutions of all types reported on their available services. Most reported counseling services and academic tutors; about two-thirds reported developmental reading, writing, and mathematics courses. Fewer than half reported that counselors had specific knowledge about learning disabilities or taped textbooks, remedial courses, diagnostic assessment, or support groups for students with special needs. The services specifically targeting students with physical or learning disabilities were more often found in the large state universities or 4-year colleges, which, according to the perceptions of the LD teachers, would be appropriate for only a small percentage of the students. Crossover students undoubtedly were well represented in that small group, but the reported pattern of services led the authors to conclude that the institutions that serve, or should serve, the most students with learning disabilities had, at that time, developed the fewest services.

A more recent national study supported the pattern of enrollment suggested by the Ohio data. Fairweather and Shaver (1991) conducted interviews with the parents of 1,242 exceptional youths representing all disabilities. They found that only 17.1% of the youths with learning disabilities attended any postsecondary course (8.5% enrolled in a vocational course, 6.8% in a 2-year course, and 1.8% in a 4-year course). By contrast, 27.8% of the students with visual impairments in this group were enrolled in a 4-year course, and about 56% of nondisabled youth. The authors concluded that the percentage of individuals with disabilities who receive postsecondary education must increase, as must our knowledge about the role postsecondary experiences play in long-term success for adults with learning disability.

Some crossover students may not be ready for postsecondary education immediately after high school. Others may never choose it. Those who have not mastered independence or lack social skills may need to prolong adolescence or engage in entry-level jobs before such a decision is made. Although traditional, it is not mandatory to enter into higher education at age 18. As observed earlier, the young person who is not a full partner in the decision-making process will most likely not be a successful college student. Time may help to overcome immaturity, but it is not a panacea. Unfortunately, once the support of the high school staff is terminated, parents and children locked into prolonged dependency may have limited access to professionals who can help them overcome this pattern. This underscores the importance of career education and counseling throughout the early school years.

THE CROSSOVER ADULT

Some crossover adults will fail to achieve vocational and emotional stability, but most will become part of the mainstream. This writer has worked with a neurologist whose childhood reading problems led to a specialization in learning disabilities. She has also tutored a veterinarian whose slow reading rate continued to cause him concern in spite of his obvious academic achievement. As mentioned previously, biographies or news reports about celebrities or local role models with learning disabilities may provide important support for the struggling adolescent or adult. More important, they should be shared with the younger crossover child before patterns of discouragement develop. Developing self-confidence; hearing, heeding, and valuing the "different drummer"; or counterbalancing poor academics with achievement in other areas are themes worth emphasizing to crossover children as soon as they can understand their relevance.

SUMMARY

We must share responsibility to make sure that each crossover child matures to become an achieving adult. Balancing support and letting go, allowing entrance into college preparatory courses, providing good information about career choices, and searching for an appropriate postsecondary setting are activities in which parents and educators must cooperate if the crossover adult is to have an opportunity to live life fully.

References

Berger, S. (1994).*College planning for gifted students* (2nd ed.). Reston, VA: The Council for Exceptional Children.

Bireley, M., Landers, M. F., Schlaerth, P., & Vernooy, J. (1986). The Wright State University Program for learning disabled students: Implications of the first decade. *Journal of Reading, Writing, and Learning Disabilities, 2,* 349–357.

Bireley, M., & Manley, E. (1980). The learning disabled student in a college environment: A report of the Wright State University's program. *Journal of Learning Disabilities, 13,* 7–10.

Brier, N. (1989). The relationship between learning disability and delinquency: A review and reappraisal. *Journal of Learning Disabilities, 22,* 546–553.

Briggs, K., & Myers, I. (1977). *Myers-Briggs Type Indicator.* Palo Alto, CA: Consulting Psychologists Press.

Brinckerhoff, L., Shaw, S., & McGuire, J. (1992). Promoting access, accommodations, and independence for college students with learning disabilities. *Journal of Learning Disabilities, 25,* 417–429.

Fairweather, J., & Shaver, D. (1991). Making the transition to postsecondary education and training. *Exceptional Children, 57,* 264–270.

Frey, D. (1991). Psychosocial needs of the gifted adolescent. In M. Bireley & J. Genshaft (Eds.), *Understanding the gifted adolescent: Educational, developmental, and multicultural issues* (pp.35–39). New York: Teachers College Press.

Huntington, D., & Bender, W. (1993). Adolescents with learning disabilities at risk? Emotional well-being, depression, suicide. *Journal of Learning Disabilities, 26,* 159–166.

Janos, Paul (1994). Counseling academically behaving adolescents about wellness. In J. Genshaft, M. Bireley, & C. Hollinger (Eds.), *Serving gifted and talented students: A resource for school personnel* (pp. 323–336). Austin, TX: Pro-Ed.

Kowalchuk, B., & King, J. (1989). Adult suicide versus coping with nonverbal learning disorder. *Journal of Learning Disabilities, 22,* 177–179.

Larson, K. (1988). A research review and alternative hypothesis explaining the link between learning disability and delinquency. *Journal of Learning Disabilities, 21,* 357–363.

Mangrum, C., & Strichart, S. (1984). *College and the learning disabled student.* Orlando, FL: Grune & Stratton.

Michael, R. (1987). Evaluating the college of choice. *Academic Therapy, 22,* 485–488.

Minskoff, E., Sautter, S., Sheldon, K., Steidle, E., & Baker, D. (1988). A comparison of learning disabled adults and high school students. *Learning Disabilities Research, 3,* 115–123.

Myers, I., & McCaulley, M. (1985). *Manual: A guide to the development and use of the Myers-Briggs Type Indicator.* Palo Alto, CA: Consulting Psychologists Press.

Nelson, R., & Lignugaris/Kraft, B. (1989). Postsecondary education for students with learning disabilities. *Journal of Learning Disabilities, 56,* 246–265.

Patton, J., & Polloway, E. (1992). Learning disability: The challenges of adulthood. *Journal of Learning Disabilities, 25,* 410–415, 447.

Sabatino, D., Miller, T., & Schmidt, C. (1981). *Learning disabilities: Systemizing teaching and service delivery.* Rockville, MD: Aspen.

Scott, S. (1994). Determining reasonable academic adjustments for college students with learning disabilities. *Journal of Learning Disabilities, 27,* 403–412.

Shaywitz, S., & Shaw, R. (1988). The admissions process: An approach to selecting learning disabled students at the most selective colleges. *Learning Disabilities Focus, 3,* 81–86.

Snyder, D., Bireley, M., Jones, D., Marra, L., & Scholl, S. (1986). *Postsecondary educational needs and current available services for learning disabled students in Ohio.* Dayton: Delta Kappa Gamma International, Alpha Delta State.

Stone, W., & La Greca, A. (1990). The social status of children with learning disabilities: A reexamination. *Journal of Learning Disabilities, 23,* 32–37.

Tieger, P. D., & Barron-Tieger, B. (1992). *Do what you are: Discover the perfect career for you through the secrets of personality type.* Boston: Little, Brown.

Appendixes

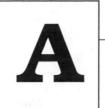

Journals and Publishing Companies with Resources for Students Who Are Gifted and Learning Disabled

JOURNALS

Gifted

Gifted Children Monthly
Gifted and Talented Publications
213 Hollydell Drive
Sewell, NJ 08080
Parent newsletter; includes activities for children.

Gifted Child Quarterly
1155 15th Street, N.W., Suite 1002
Washington, DC 20005
Part of membership of National Association for Gifted Children; research oriented.

Gifted Child Today Magazine
Prufrock Press
P.O. Box 8813
Waco, TX 76714-8813
Teacher/parent-oriented research and ideas.

Journal for the Education of the Gifted
The Council for Exceptional Children;
1920 Association Drive
Reston, VA 22091

Part of membership of gifted division of the Council for Exceptional Children; research oriented

Journal of Creative Behavior
Creative Education Foundation
State University College
1300 Elmwood Avenue
Buffalo, NY 14222
Emphasis on creativity topics

The Journal of Secondary Gifted Education
Prufrock Press
P.O. Box 8813
Waco, TX 76714-8813
Emphasis on secondary gifted education

Roeper Review
Roeper City and Country School
P.O. Box 329
Bloomfield Hills, MI 48303
Research oriented

Understanding Our Gifted
Open Space Communications
P.O. Box 18268
Boulder, CO 80308-8268
Practical information on social, emotional, and intellectual needs of gifted individuals.

Learning Disabilities

Intervention in School and Clinic
(formerly *Academic Therapy*)
Pro-Ed
8700 Shoal Creek Boulevard
Austin, TX 78758-6897
Teacher-oriented management and teaching strategies.

Journal of Learning Disabilities
Pro-Ed
8700 Shoal Creek Boulevard.
Austin, TX 78758-6897
Research oriented

LDA Newsbriefs
LDA
4156 Library Road.
Pittsburgh, PA 15234
Part of membership of Learning Disabilities Association of America; short items of interest to parents, educators, and other professionals.

Learning Disabilities Research and Practice
The Council for Exceptional Children
1920 Association Drive
Reston, Va 22091
Part of membership of LD division of CEC; research practice and political activism orientation

Learning Disability Quarterly
Council for Learning Disabilities
P.O. Box 40403
Overland Park, KS 66204
Part of membership of Council for LD; research oriented

General

Exceptional Children
The Council for Exceptional Children
1920 Association Drive
Reston, VA 22091
Part of membership of CEC; research and political activism orientation; all exceptionalities including gifted.

TEACHING Exceptional Children
The Council for Exceptional Children
1920 Association Dr.
Reston, VA 22091
Part of membership of CEC; classroom management and curriculum orientation

PUBLISHERS OF MATERIALS

Enrichment

Center for Creative Learning
P.O. Box 619
Honeoye, NY 14471
Creative problem-solving materials and consultants.

Creative Learning Consultants
1610 Brook Lynn Drive
Beavercreek, OH 45432
Curriculum enrichment and consultants.

Creative Learning Process
P.O. Box 320
Mansfield Center, CT 06250
Enrichment materials; software; Renzulli products and training.

D.O.K. Publishers
P.O. Box 605
East Aurora, NY 14052
Creative problem solving; futures; thinking skills; enrichment for content subjects.

Engine-Uity Ltd.
P.O. Box 9610
Phoenix, AZ 85068
Ready-to-use learning centers; language arts and content areas.

Free Spirit Publishing
400 First Avenue North
Suite 616-13
Minneapolis, MN 55401-1724
Books about typical problems written for gifted students to read.

Good Apple
1204 Buchanan
P.O. Box 29
Carthage, IL 62321-0299
Enrichment materials, especially in language arts.

INTERACT
P.O. Box 997-Y90
Lakeside, CA 92040
Simulations in content areas for elementary and secondary school students.

Learning Links Inc.
2300 Marcus Avenue
New Hyde Park, NY 11042
Literature-based "topic-ties" or lists of books that address a given topic.

Midwest Publications
P.O. Box 448, Dept. 17
Pacific Grove, CA 93950
Workbooks addressing a variety of thinking skills.

Trillium Press
First Avenue
Unionville, NY 10988
Enrichment materials; thinking skills.

Zephyr Press
3316 North Chapel Avenue
P.O. Box 13448-M
Tucson, AZ 85732-3448
Books and learning packets on thinking skills, affective topics, and content topics.

Intervention

Barnell-Loft
958 Church Street
Baldwin, NY 11510
Reading kits: reading skill-building material.

Beckley-Cardy
1900 North Narragansett
Chicago, IL 60639
Concrete and written materials for basic skills.

Curriculum Associates
5 Esquire Road
North Billerica, MA 01862-9987
Supplemental/diagnostic reading and math skills.

Dale Seymour Publications
P.O. Box 10888
Palo Alto, CA 94303
Supplemental reading, math, thinking skills.

DLM Teaching Resources
P.O. Box 4000
One DLM Park
Allen, TX 75002
Supplemental math and reading; software.

Edmark Associates
655 South Orcas Street
Seattle, WA 98018
Early childhood; math and reading; software

Educational Teaching Aids
159 West Kinzie Street
Chicago, IL 60610
Concrete materials for teaching reading
and math.

Recordings for the Blind
214 East 58th Street
New York, NY 10022
Taped materials.

Research Press Catalogue
Dept. B
2612 North Mattis Avenue
Champaign, IL 61821
Books and videos on behavioral
management; social skill development;
special education issues.

Special Times
Cambridge Developmental Lab, Inc.
86 West Street
Waltham, MA 02154
K–8 software; 100 titles specifically for
LD; in content areas, word processing,
and thinking skills.

Organizations that Serve Students Who Are Gifted or Learning Disabled

Gifted

The Council for Exceptional Children
The Association for the Gifted (TAG) Division
1920 Association Drive
Reston, VA 22091
Parent and professional.

World Council for Gifted and Talented, Inc.
Purdue University
1446 South Campus Courts-Building G
West Lafayette, IN 47097-1446
International professional membership.

National Association for Gifted Children
5100 North Edgewood Drive
St. Paul, MN 551112
Parent and professional.

Learning Disabilities

The Council for Exceptional Children
Division for Learning Disabilities (DLD)
1920 Association Drive
Reston, VA 22091
Professional.

Learning Disabilities Association of America
4156 Library Road
Pittsburgh, PA 15234
Parent and professional.

Council for Learning Disabilities
P.O. Box 40403
Overland Park, KS 66214
Professional.

Orton Dyslexia Society
724 York Road
Baltimore, MD 21240
Parent and professional.

C

Elementary and Secondary Computer Programs

WORD PROCESSING/CREATIVE WRITING

Program Name	Grades	Producer[1]	Hardware
Author! Author!	1 up	MIN-P	Apple II series
Bank Street StoryBook	3–9	MIN-5	Apple II series; Commodore; IBM; Tandy
Bank Street Writer (Broderbund Version)	2 up	BR	128K Apple II series, IBM PC jr. PS/2
Bank Street Writer III	2–12	SCH	Apple II series; IBM; Tandy
Be a Writer!	1–3	SUN	Apple II series
FrEd Writer	3 up	CUE	64K Apple II series
Kid Writer	2–6	SP	Apple II series; IBM; Commodore
Language Experience	K up	FB	Apple II series
MacWrite II	K–8	CL	128K Apple II series; 256K IBM PC, PC jr; PS/2 with color graphics card
Magic Slate II	2 up	SUN	128K Apple II series
MECC Write Start	6–10	MECC	64K Apple II, IIe, IIc, IIGS
MECC Writer	4–12	MECC	64K Apple II series
Medley	6 up	MIL	Apple IIGS
Mercury	3 up	MECC	Apple IIGS
Multiscribe GS	6–12	CL	768 Apple IIGS
My Words	5–8	HA	64K Apple IIe, IIc with ECHO or Cricket speech synthesizer
Sensible Grammar	6 up	SE	128K Apple IIe (with 80 column card), IIc, IIGS
Text Tiger	3–12	MIN-P	Apple II series
Snoopy Writer	1–4	RA	64K Apple IIe, IIc, IIGS
Talking Text Writer	Pre-K–6	SCH	128K Apple II series IBM PC Requires ECHO or Cricket
Writing Workshop	4 up	MIL	Apple II series

[1]See attached references for complete name of producer.

Typing/Keyboarding

Program Name	Grades	Producer[1]	Hardware
Alphabetic Keyboarding	6 up	SW	Apple II series; IBM; Tandy
Keyboard Cadet	K–6	MIN	Apple II series
Kids on Keys	Pre-K–4	SP	48 Apple II series; Commodore 64/128; 128K IBM PC, AT with color graphics card; Tandy 1000
Mavis Beacon Teaches Typing	1up	SO	Apple II series, GS; *Typing* Commodore Amiga, 64/128; IBM; Atari ST.
Sticky Bear Typing	1 up	WR	Apple II series; Commodore; IBM, Tandy
Success with Typing	5–12	SCH	Apple II series; IBM; Tandy
Type!	5–12	BR	64K Apple II series 128K IBM PC, PCjr, PS/2; Macintosh 512, PLUS, SE; Tandy 1000
Type to Learn	3 up	SUN	Apple II series
Typing Tutor IV	6 up	S&S	Apple II series; Commodore; IBM
Typing Well	3 up	MI	Apple II series

Key to Companies

BR—-Broderbund Software
P.O. Box 12947
San Rafael, CA 94913-2947

CL—Claris Corporation
440 Clyde Avenue
Mountain View, CA 04943

CUE—CUE Softswap
P.O. Box 271704
Concord, CA 94527-1704

FB—First Byte
3333 East Spring Street, Suite 302
Long Beach, CA 90806

HA—Hartley Courseware
Box 419
Dimondale, MI 48821

LC—Learning Company
6493 Kaiser Drive
Fremont, CA 94555

MECC—MECC
3490 Lexington, N.
St. Paul, MN 55126

MIL—-Milliken Publishing
1100 Research Boulevard
PO Box 21579
St. Louis, MO 63132-0579

MIN—P Mindplay
100 Conifer Hill Drive
Building 3, Suite 301
Danvers, MA 01923

MIN-S—Mindscape
3444 Dundee Road
Northbrook, IL 60062

RA—Random House
400 Hahn Road
Westminster, MD 21157

SCH—Scholastic, Inc.
2931 East McCarty Street
P.O. Box 7502
Jefferson City, MO 65102

S&S—Simon & Schuster
1 Gulf & Western Plaza
New York, NY 10023

SE—Sensible Software
335 East Big Beaver, Suite 207
Troy, MI 48083

SO—Software Toolworks
One Toolworks Plaza
13557 Venture Boulevard
Sherman Oaks, CA 91423

SP—Spinnaker Software Co.
1 Kendall Square
Cambridge, MA 02139

SW—South-Western Publishing Co.
5101 Madison Road.
Cincinnati, OH 45227

SU—Sunburst Communications
39 Washington Avenue
Pleasantville, NY 10570-9971

WR Weekly Reader Software
Optimum Resource, Inc.
10 Station Place
Norfolk, VA 06058

Information taken from:

International Council for Computers in Education (1989). *The 1989 educational software preview guide.* Eugene, OR: The Council.

Neill, S., & Neill, G. (1989). *Only the best: The discriminating software guide for preschool–grade 12.* New York: Education News Service.

Neill, S., & Neill, G. (1991). *The annual guide to highest-rated educational software: Only the best: Preschool–Grade 12.* New York: R.R. Bowker.

D

Bibliography on the Crossover Condition and Related Issues

Baldwin, L., & Garguilo, D. (1983). A model program for elementary-age learning disabled/gifted youngsters. In L. Fox, L. Brody, & D. Tobin (Eds.), *Learning disabled/ gifted children: Identification and programming* (pp. 207–222). Baltimore: University Park Press.

Baum, S. (1984). Meeting the needs of learning disabled gifted students. *Roeper Review, 7,* 16–19.

Baum, S. (1988). An enrichment program for gifted learning disabled students. *Gifted Child Quarterly, 32,* 226–230.

Baum, S., & Owen, S. (1988). High ability/learning disabled students: How are they different? *Gifted Child Quarterly, 32,* 321–326.

Bireley, M., & Hoehn, L. (1988). Mental processing preferences in gifted children. *Journal of the Illinois Council of the Gifted, 7,* 28–31.

Bireley, M., Languis, M., & Williamson, T. (1992). Physiological uniqueness: A new perspective on the learning disabled/gifted child. *Roeper Review, 14,* 101–107.

Brown, S., & Yakimowski, M. (1987). Intelligence scores of gifted students on the WISC-R. *Gifted Child Quarterly, 31,* 130–134.

Clampit, M., & SIlver, S. (1986). Four tables for the statistical interpretation of factor scores on the Wechsler Intelligence Scale for Children-Revised (WISC-R). *Journal of School Psychology, 24,* 395–404.

Clearinghouse on Handicapped and Gifted Children. (1990). *Giftedness and the gifted: What's it all about?* (ERIC Digest #E476). Reston, VA: The Council for Exceptional Children.

Clearinghouse on Handicapped and Gifted Children. (1990). *Gifted but learning disabled: A puzzling paradox.* (ERIC Digest #479). Reston, VA: The Council for Exceptional Children.

Clearinghouse on Handicapped and Gifted Children. (1990). *Underachieving gifted students.* (ERIC Digest #E478). Reston, VA: The Council for Exceptional Children.

Daniels, P. (1983). *Teaching the gifted/learning disabled child.* Rockville, MD: Aspen.

Davis, G. (1994). Identifying the creatively gifted. In J. Genshaft, M. Bireley, & C. Hollinger (Eds.), *Serving the gifted and talented: A resource for school personnel* (pp. 67–82). Austin, TX: Pro-Ed.

Fisher, D., & Frankfurter, A. (1977). Normal and disabled readers can locate and identify letters: Where's the perceptual deficit? *Journal of Reading Behavior, 9,* 167–175.

Fox, L., Brody, L, & Tobin, D. (Eds.), (1983). *Learning disabled/gifted children: Identification and programming.* Baltimore: University Park Press.

Hallowell, E., & Ratey, J. (1994). *Driven to distraction.* New York: Pantheon.

Hoehn, L., & Bireley, M. (1987). Learning styles: Teaching implications for average and bright learning disabled children. *Academic Therapy, 22,* 437–441.

Languis, M. (1986). *Brain mapping and the study of learning disability.* Paper presented at Topographic Brain Mapping and Evoked Potential Seminar, Bio-Logic Systems Corporation, Chicago.

Languis, M. (1988, April). *Brain mapping research report: Developmental and group differences in the auditory evoked potential (AEP 300) task.* Paper presented at the meeting of the American Educational Research Association, Chicago.

Languis, M. (1995, April). *Visual processing patterns in middle school learning disabled students.* Paper presented at the meeting of the American Educational Research Association, San Francisco.

Languis, M., Bireley, M., Brigner, L., & Holland S. (1990, March). *Topographic brain mapping assessment of cognitive processing patterns in four groups of learners.* Paper presented at the meeting of the Ohio Association for Gifted Children, Columbus.

Languis, M., & Wittrock, M. (1986). Integrating neuropsychological and cognitive research: A perspective for bridging brain behavior relationships. In J. Obrzut & G. Hynd (Eds.), *Child neuropsychology Vol.1: Theory and research* (pp. 209–239). New York: Academic.

Lerner, J. (1985). *Learning disabilities: Theories, diagnosis, and teaching strategies.* Boston: Houghton Mifflin.

Luria, A. (1980). *Higher cortical functions in man (2nd ed.).* New York: Basic Books.

Maker, J. (1977). *Providing programs for the gifted handicapped.* Reston, VA: The Council for Exceptional Children.

Morrison, M., & Dungan, R. (1991). *The identification of creative thinking ability: A multifactored approach.* Upper Arlington, OH: Upper Arlington City Schools.

Naour, P., & Languis, M. (1986). *Brain mapping assessment of learning disability at two developmental levels.* Columbus: Challenge Grant, Ohio Board of Regents.

Piirto, J. (1994). *Talented children and adults: Their development and education.* New York: Merrill.

Polloway, E., Schewel, R., & Patton, J. (1992). Learning disabilities in adulthood: Personal perspectives. *Journal of Learning Disabilities, 25,* 520–522.

Renzulli, J. (1986). The three-ring conception of giftedness: A developmental model for creative productivity. In R. Sternberg & J. Davidson (Eds.), *Conceptions of giftedness* (pp. 53–92). Cambridge, England: Cambridge University Press.

Sattler, J. (1992). *Assessment of children's intelligence and special abilities* (3rd ed.). San Diego: Sattler.

Schiff, M. Kaufman, A., & Kaufman, N. (1981). Scatter analysis of WISC-R profiles for learning disabled children with superior intelligence. *Journal of Learning Disabilites, 14,* 400–404.

Silver, L. (1990). Attention deficit-hyperactivity disorder: Is it a learning disability or a related disorder? *Journal of Learning Disabilities, 23,* 394–397.

Silver, S., & Clampit, M. (1990). WISC-R profiles of high ability children: Interpretation of verbal-performance discrepancies. *Gifted Child Quarterly, 34,* 76–79.

Silverman, L. (1989). Invisible gifts, invisible handicaps. *Roeper Review, 12,* 37–42.

Udall, A., & Maker, C. J. (1983). A pilot program for elementary-age learning disabled/gifted students. In L. Fox, L. Brody, & D. Tobin (Eds.), *Learning disabled/gifted children: Identification and programming* (pp. 223–242). Baltimore: University Park Press.

Vail, P. (1987). *Smart kids with school problems: Things to know and ways to help.* New York: Dutton.

Vespi, L., & Yewchuk, C. (1992). A phenomenological study of the social/emotional characteristics of gifted learning disabled children. *Journal for the Education of the Gifted, 16,* 55–72.

Webb, J., & Latimer, D. (1993, July). ADHD and children who are gifted. *(ERIC Digest* (EDO-EC-93-5). Reston, VA: The Council for Exceptional Children.

Webb, J. (1994, June). Nurturing social-emotional development of gifted children. *(ERIC Digest* EDO-EC-93-10). Reston, VA: The Council for Exceptional Children.

Weiss, G., & Hechtman, L. (1986). *Hyperactive children grown up.* New York: Guilford.

Whitmore, J. (1980). *Giftedness, conflict, and underachievement.* Boston: Allyn & Bacon.

CEC Teacher Resources

Crossover Children: A Sourcebook for Helping Children Who Are Gifted and Learning Disabled, Second Edition
by Marlene Bireley
A rich resource that provides specific strategies to help children who are gifted and learning disabled and/or ADD control impulsivity, increase attention, enhance memory, improve social skills, and develop a positive self-concept. It also provides recommendations for academic interventions and enrichment activities.

No. P5121. 1995. 94 pp. ISBN 0-86586-264-8
Regular Price $28.00   CEC Member Price $19.60

Back Off, Cool Down, Try Again: Teaching Students How to Control Aggressive Behavior
by Sylvia Rockwell
A vividly descriptive primer on how to nurture the social development of students with aggressive behavior in a classroom setting using the stages of group development as the basis for classroom management. The focus moves from teacher control to control through peer interaction. Strategies for group management, affective and academic instruction, and planning, documentation, and consultation are presented.

No. P5120. 1995. 144 pp. ISBN 0-86586-263-X
Regular Price $27.00   CEC Member Price $19.00

Tough to Reach, Tough to Teach: Students with Behavior Problems
by Sylvia Rockwell
Through the use of anecdotes, the author prepares teachers for the shock of abusive language and hostile behavior in the classroom. This book will allow you to have a plan for meeting the challenges of teaching these students more effective ways to communicate. Provides many practical management strategies for defusing and redirecting disruptive behavior.

No. P387. 1993. 106 pp. ISBN 0-86586-235-4
Regular Price $22.00   CEC Member Price $15.40

Integrating Transition Planning into the IEP Process
by Lynda L. West, Stephanie Corbey, Arden Boyer-Stephens, Bonnie Jones, Robert J. Miller, Mickey Sarkees-Wircenski
Shows how to incorporate transition planning into the IEP process. Helps students become self-advocates. Describes skills needed for employment, community living, postsecondary education, and leisure activities. Includes three sample IEPs.

No. P386. 1992. 78 pp. ISBN 0-86586-222-2
Regular Price $15.70   CEC Member Price $11.00

Survival Guide for the First-Year Special Education Teacher, Revised Edition
by Mary Kemper Cohen, Maureen Gale, and Joyce M. Meyer
Tips for new teachers to start you off on the right foot. Tells how to get organized, how to get to know the students, how to get along with co-workers and parents, and how to take care of yourself.

No. P335R. 1994. 48 pp. ISBN 0-86586-256-7
Regular Price $12.00   CEC Member Price $8.40

Resourcing: Handbook for Special Education Resource Teachers
by Mary Yeomans Jackson
Gives special education teachers the help they need to fill new roles outside the self-contained classroom. Shows how to be the best resource to other teachers, administrators, community agencies, students, and parents. Written by a practitioner who knows how to make it work.

No. P366. 1992. 64 pp. ISBN 0-86586-219-2
Regular Price $12.00   CEC Member Price $8.40

Prices may change without notice.

Send orders to: The Council for Exceptional Children, Dept. K50750, 1920 Association Drive, Reston, VA 22091-1589. 1-800-CEC-READ.